Boston, Lincolnshire

Historic North Sea port and market town

Boston, Lincolnshire

Historic North Sea port and market town

John Minnis and Katie Carmichael
with Clive Fletcher and Mary Anderson

Published by Historic England, The Engine House, Fire Fly Avenue, Swindon SN2 2EH
www.HistoricEngland.org.uk

Historic England is a Government service championing England's heritage and giving expert, constructive advice, and, the English Heritage Trust is a charity caring for the National Heritage Collection of more than 400 historic properties and their collections.

First published 2015

ISBN 978-1-84802-270-6

British Library Cataloguing in Publication data
A CIP catalogue record for this book is available from the British Library.

For more information about images from the Archive, contact Archives Services Team, Historic England, The Engine House, Fire Fly Avenue, Swindon SN2 2EH; telephone (01793) 414600.

Brought to publication by Jess Ward, Publishing, Historic England.

Typeset in Georgia Pro Light 9.25/13pt

Edited by Susan Kelleher
Page layout by Hybert Design
Printed in the Czech Republic via Akcent Media Limited.

Front cover
The long straight waterways, the red-brick cottages with their white sash windows and pantiled roofs and, above all, the presence of Maud Foster Mill are some of the elements that have led many observers to liken Boston to towns in the Low Countries.
[DP165381]

Inside front cover
Boston, showing the docks and the principal routes into the town.

Frontispiece
South Street, seen from the Town Bridge, is at the heart of Boston's maritime past. Warehouses flank the quayside and the Customs House of 1725 is in the background.
[DP165480]

Acknowledgements
Many Boston buildings from the late 18th century until the 1860s had a distinctive design of lintel with a moulded keystone, as seen on this example from Nos 14–16 South Street, which also incorporates a pair of unusual incised diamond motifs.
[DP160497]

Inside back cover
The classic view of the 'Boston Stump' from the Town Bridge has been enhanced by the new St Botolph's footbridge.
[DP151255]

Contents

Acknowledgements

This book is based on fieldwork and research conducted by Katie Carmichael and John Minnis. Kathryn Morrison kindly read the manuscript and offered useful comments. Clive Fletcher prepared the final chapter and commented on the text. Ben Robinson also read part of the text. Richard Hewlings offered his unpublished research on Boston's 18th- and early 19th-century public buildings. Luke Jacob carried out research into Shodfriars Hall. Pat Payne took the majority of the photographs with some contributed by Derek Kendall and aerial views were by David MacLeod. Allan Adams made the drawing of the Guildhall and Philip Sinton produced the maps. Nigel Wilkins provided images from the Historic England Archives. The Designation team in Cambridge kindly made available material gathered as part of a Defined Area Survey of Boston.

Our greatest debt is to Neil Wright, who has spent many years researching and writing about Boston. In addition to our drawing upon his books and articles on the town, Neil very kindly made his unpublished research available to us and has read the manuscript, making many helpful comments.

We would also like to specially thank Adrian Wilkinson at Lincolnshire Archives who went out of his way to help us with the Sherwin Roberts drawings collection. Professor Stephen Rigby kindly made his articles on medieval Boston available to us.

We gained much help in Boston from local residents who supplied us with photographs, let us visit their houses and premises, and generally gave encouragement. They include Val Aaron, Terry Anthony, John Bird, Colleen Kitchen, Brian Mason and Pat Pomeroy. Also, we would like to thank Liz Bates at Heritage Lincolnshire, Alison Fairman at Boston Preservation Trust and Caroline Wallis at Coastal Boston.

We received support from Boston Borough Council which helped to publicise the project and we would like to thank Steve Lumb, Head of Built Environment and Development, and Luke Skerritt at Boston Guildhall Museum. We had some useful conversations with Mary Anderson of Anderson & Glenn, Conservation Architects, and she had input into the final chapter, as Boston Borough Council's conservation adviser.

Foreword

Unmistakable and striking, rising magnificently above the landscape of the fens, the famous tower of St Botolph's Church – the 'Boston Stump' – can be seen from miles and miles away.

It almost shouts, "Welcome to Boston – come in – you are here". The same sight greets travellers now, just as it has done for generations, with the Wednesday and Saturday markets in full flow and the Market Place buzzing with colour, life and people. Boston has an impressive history and heritage, great spaces, fabulous architecture, rich archaeology and a layout that escaped the worst excesses of 'comprehensive redevelopment' in the 1960s and 1970s. The eclectic mix of historic buildings, curious lanes and the commanding parish church define a town on the very edge of England, away from the main road systems, quietly getting on with itself – and, until recently underselling its important past – and its magnificent heritage.

In terms of trade with Europe, the medieval importance of Boston was second only to London, with magnificent buildings demonstrating the power and wealth of the town and port. The market place and street pattern evolved with later additions, veneers and frontages reflecting subsequent fortunes of the town. St Botolph's, with its 272ft (82.9m) lantern tower, the 14th-century St Mary's Guildhall, Tudor timber-framed buildings through to fine Georgian shopfronts and 19th-century riverside warehousing, are all symbolic of the town's great past, contributed by successive generations. Boston's distinctive townscape and iconic waterways are now recognised as the bedrock of the town's future prosperity, well-being and aspiration.

We are delighted to introduce this celebration of Boston's historic significance. It is fitting that this is the first in the new series of *Informed Conservation* published by Historic England – the public body that champions and protects England's historic places.

Sir Laurie Magnus
Chairman, Historic England

Steve Lumb
Head of Built Environment and Development, Boston Borough Council

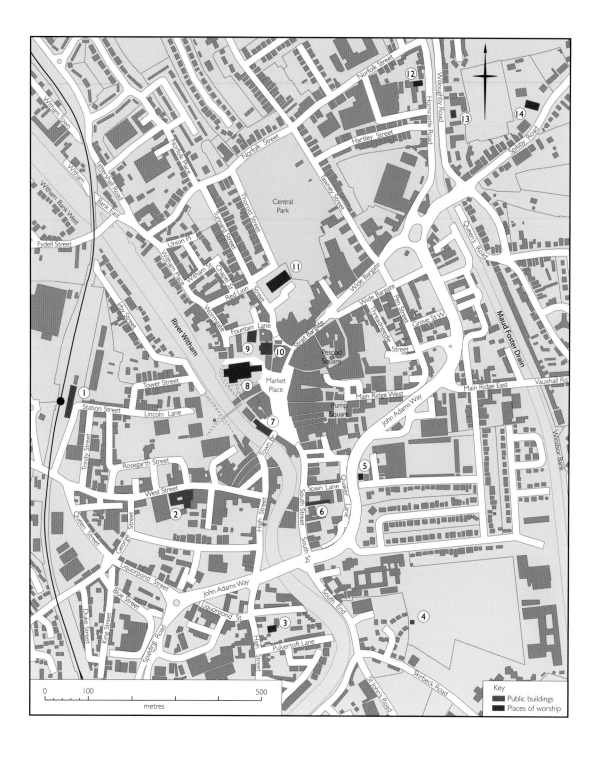

Witham Town

Witham

Tattershall Road

Witham Bank West

Witham Bank East

Fydell Street

River Witham

Irby Street

Trinity Street

Station Street

Lincoln Lane

Tower Street

Rosegarth Street

Queen Street

George Street

West Street

Liquorpond Street

Blue Street

Duke Street

King Street

Spalding Road

John Adams Way

Liquorpond St

Pulvertoft Lane

High Street

High Street

South Sq

South End

St John's Road

Skirbeck Road

Norfolk Place

Norfolk Street

Thorold Street

Union Pl

Witham Place

Witham St

Chapel St

Tunnard Street

Red Lion Street

Wormgate

Fountain Lane

Strait Bargate

Market Place

Town Br

Central Park

Tawney Street

Hartley Street

Norfolk Bargate

Willoughby Road

Horncastle Road

Spilsby Road

Wide Bargate

Wide Bargate

Pen Street

Threadneedle Street

Grove St W

Pescod Square

Pump Square

Main Ridge West

Main Ridge East

Vauxhall Rd

John Adams Way

Queen's Road

Maud Foster Drain

Windsor Bank

Spain Lane

South Street

Quaker Lane

1

2

3

4

5

6

7

8

9

10

11

12

13

14

Key
Public buildings
Places of worship

0   100   500

metres

Introduction

Boston impresses above all by its remoteness. Many visitors to the town have commented on how the great tower (known as 'the Stump') of St Botolph's Church (at 272ft (82.9m), the tallest of any parish church in England) stands out like a beacon across the flat expanses of that part of Lincolnshire known as Holland.

Comparisons with Holland have gone beyond the name. As A E Richardson pointed out in his 1921 *Architectural Review* essay on the town, 'Almost every visitor to Boston begins by comparing the place to Dutch towns of similar size, a resemblance, almost an illusion, heightened to an extraordinary degree by the adjacent waterways, the windmills and the neat brick houses.'[1] The resemblance was so strong that Boston stood in convincingly for the Netherlands in Powell and Pressburger's wartime film, *One of our Aircraft is Missing* (1942). The red-brick and pantiled buildings in the Wormgate area definitely have a Dutch flavour to them.

Yet, despite a passing resemblance to somewhere in the Low Countries with its great town church located on the edge of an enormous market place, Boston is essentially an English town with a wealth of fine architecture from the medieval period to the 19th century. The key aspect in the town's history is its role as a medieval port, the second most important in England, which made it, for a time, one of the richest provincial towns.

Boston's subsequent history has been one of decline and resurgence – a long decline after its heyday as a port and then a renaissance in the late 18th century when the draining of the nearby fens and straightening of the River Witham allowed the town, once again, to handle much of the commercial business of Lincolnshire.

In the late 19th and early 20th centuries, Boston was often visited for its ancient buildings and, increasingly, as a place of pilgrimage for Americans investigating their past. Boston was unique in providing not just the name of Boston, Massachusetts, but its leaders for the first 50 years of its existence. Almost a third of Boston's citizens sailed on the *Arbella* in 1630 to seek religious freedom in the New World. These roots led to practical support for the town when $55,000 was raised from the United States to pay for the strengthening of the tower of St Botolph's and other repairs to the church between 1928 and 1933. In 1938, an American Room in Boston's finest house, Fydell House, was opened by the American Ambassador Joseph Kennedy, father of John F Kennedy.

Places of worship and buildings open to the public.

KEY

1 Railway Station
2 Municipal Buildings
3 General Baptist Chapel
4 Hussey Tower
5 Unitarian Chapel
6 St Mary's Guildhall
7 Assembly Room
8 St Botolph's Church
9 Sessions House
10 Public Library
11 Centenary Methodist Chapel
12 St Mary's Roman Catholic Church
13 Maud Foster Mill
14 Holy Trinity Church

The town was depicted in the line drawings of F L Griggs as an almost unbelievably romantic place of ancient buildings and quaint alleys with the hint of seafaring in every vista. In 1930 Boston was described as 'a very compact little town, exceedingly healthy, clean and well lighted, having a business quarter furnished with attractive, modern shops and residential quarters well laid out and pleasing to look upon'.[2] Looking at aerial photographs of the town taken the same year, it is the compactness of Boston that is so striking (*see* Fig 2). Land ownership by the Fydells ensured that fields extended almost to South Square and in no direction was the town more than about 15 minutes walk from open country. Later in the 1930s, and especially from the 1960s, Boston extended far beyond its historic boundaries.

Today, Boston is changing again after a long period of stagnation. An ill-considered inner relief road in the 1970s did much harm to the town whilst failing to solve its traffic problems. A low wage agricultural economy meant that there was little capital investment in the town.

Boston remains little understood, architecturally. Nicholas Antram, who revised the Lincolnshire volume in the Pevsner *Buildings of England* series, said that there was 'an urgent need for a detailed investigation of the buildings in the town centre'.[3] We have tried to address this within the confines of a small volume although there is still much scope for further work to be done.

The Market Place is still a scene of tremendous vitality on Wednesday and Saturday market days and St Botolph's is a focus for visitors to the town as it has been for over 500 years. But there is much more to attract both local residents and visitors should they care to look above the shopfronts and explore the many alleys and lanes that date back to medieval times. This book will highlight that half-hidden heritage.

The doorway to Tunnard House c 1790.
[John Minnis]

1

The early history of Boston

The site where Boston now stands was once part of a series of low-lying islands surrounded by semi-tidal water. Over time silting gradually connected these islands to form a chain with fens to the north and marshes to the south. Sporadic finds from the Neolithic and Bronze Age eras, and a total lack from the Iron Age, suggest that the area was not settled during these periods. The first evidence for settlement, albeit limited and probably seasonal, comes from the Roman period – Romano-British pottery, including Romano-British greyware and Nene Valley ware was found during an excavation at Boston Grammar School and it has been suggested that the fragments were briquetage, objects associated with the production of salt.[4] The pottery was deeply buried at just under half a metre above sea level, but the water table in Boston is less than 2m beneath the current ground level and deep excavation requires the continued pumping of water. Most excavation has been carried out commercially in advance of construction and only goes as deep as necessary for the proposed piles or foundations. As such it is possible that further early evidence for occupation survives, sealed beneath layers of silt. One of the benefits of having a high-water table is that the potential for the preservation of organic matter, notably leather goods, is known to be very high.

Skirbeck, today a suburb of Boston, lies to the south-east of the town centre, past the dock and the Maud Foster Drain, on the north side of the River Witham after it turns eastward. The Grade II* church of St Nicholas (Fig 1) is an ancient institution with late 13th-century arcaded nave and a 14th-century tower arch. Recorded in the Domesday Book, some have speculated that Skirbeck once included the area that would later become Boston. Two sunken-floored pit-houses (*Grubenhauser*) were excavated in the vicinity of St Nicholas School, Skirbeck, evidence of limited occupation in the 8th century, whilst a late 9th/10th-century Saxon hamlet at nearby Fishtoft was partially excavated.[5] It seems almost certain that some form of settlement existed in Boston prior to the Norman invasion of 1066, but it is after that date that the town is known to have expanded, thanks to the establishment of trade fairs.

Boston's development as a town is strongly connected to both the fairs and the church of St Botolph, from which Boston (St Botolph's Town) derives its name. The first known documentary reference to St Botolph's is a charter made in 1091 by Alan Rufus (d 1093), Earl of Richmond[6] and Brittany, whereby he granted the church to St Mary's Abbey in York.[7] However, the earliest excavated

Boston as depicted on the Gough Map of c 1375 (shown as drawn with east at the top of the map). Boston is illustrated as a sizeable unwalled town with a church (shown as a spire surmounted by a cross) straddling the River Witham and connected by roads to Bolingbroke, Wainfleet, Spalding (passing Fosdyke) and Lincoln (passing Sleaford).
[MS Gough gen top 16 © Bodleian Library, University of Oxford]

evidence for the medieval town dates from the 12th century, by which time Boston had become an important port with strong trade links to the Low Countries and inland to Lincoln.

Boston's establishment as well as its subsequent success, wealth and expansion was directly related to the surrounding waterways and the ways in which they were exploited and managed over time: Boston's relationship with the water has never been an easy one, as the archaeological and documentary records show. The first known attempt to control the watercourse was in 1121 when the Fossdyke was cleared to connect the Rivers Trent and Witham (known as the Haven where it passes through Boston town centre), creating a navigable inland route to Lincoln which greatly increased trade through Boston and linked it to vast tracts of the country beyond.[8]

The Barditch too was a significant influence on the development and layout of Boston throughout the medieval period – the substantial ditch ran from north to south, arching out to the east, and is believed to have defined the limits of the medieval town. The exact reason for its construction in the 11th or 12th century is debated. Some suggest it was defensive, others that it marked a boundary, or that it was a means of controlling access to the town and the fairs. One fact that seems certain is that it would have acted as drainage and a sewer for the town. It has been suggested that Boston was enclosed by a wall associated with the ditch but archaeological evidence is scant, and Gough's map of *c* 1375 (*see* p 4) shows it as unwalled. The Barditch, one crossing point of which was at Bargate, was later enclosed with bricks and exists, at least in part, beneath the modern town. The line of the ditch (shown on Hall's map of 1741 – *see* p 22) is partially visible in the street pattern of the town as the termination point of a number of the lanes leading east from the Market Place. The course of the Barditch in the vicinity of Bargate is not shown on any map but is generally agreed to have gone from the north-west to the south-east. Two excavations on the corner of Strait Bargate and New Street, however, raise an intriguing possibility. An excavation at No 3 New Street discovered a substantial east–west ditch in the vicinity of the expected location of the Barditch but was discounted as such due to its orientation.[9] Nearby, only 50m or so to the north-east, an excavation behind Nos 30/32 Strait Bargate also discovered a substantial ditch – measuring just under 2m deep and 3.5m wide, with 14th-century pottery in the cut layer, and apparently sealed over in the 16th century.[10] Running almost south-west to

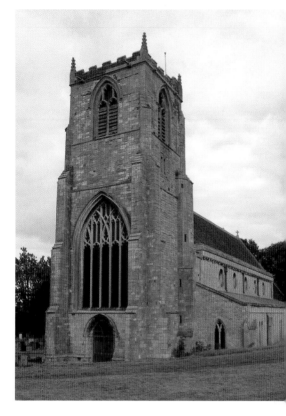

Figure 1
The church of St Nicholas, Skirbeck. The earliest part of the church dates to the 13th century but here have been many alterations and additions, including those by Sir George Gilbert Scott in 1869–75.
[John Minnis]

north-east, this was clearly a substantial ditch, likely to have been dug prior to the 14th century at which point it ceased to be routinely cleared and began to fill up. One hypothesis, given the dimensions and datable finds, is that the sections discovered formed part of the Barditch. However, once again, the orientation of the excavated ditch runs contrary to popular belief regarding the line of the Barditch – further excavation within this area may help to resolve this question.

The land beyond the Barditch was swampy and the town was constantly faced with the issue of intermittent flooding, resulting in methods of land-raising and reclamation being employed beyond the boundaries of the Barditch as early as the 12th century and throughout the medieval period. The failure to maintain the Fossdyke in the 14th century resulted in the channel through Lincoln becoming unnavigable, an event that severely affected trade in Boston.[11] In an attempt to divert excess water away from the town, the Maud Foster Gowt (Drain) was finished *c* 1569 (around the time that alterations were made to the northern outlet of the Barditch and the ditch behind Nos 30/32 Strait Bargate was filled in). Similarly, the North Forty-Foot Drain, completed *c* 1720, at first fed water back into the Witham north of Boston but in the 1760s the creation of the South Forty-Foot Drain allowed water to be drained to the south of the town as part of a wider drainage scheme across Holland Fen. However, flow through the River Witham was so reduced that the main channel now began to silt up, reducing it to such an extent that only small boats could navigate it. As a result the river was canalised to the north of the town, with a sluice at the junction with the earlier channel constructed between 1764 and 1766.[12] This helped to improve the flow of water somewhat but in 1812 a further Act of Parliament was obtained for the town centre which allowed buildings and quays projecting into the channel to be removed in order to straighten and narrow it where necessary. In the course of this work, the bend between the Grand Sluice and St Botolph's Church (visible in the layout of Wormgate, which originally followed the curve of the river) was removed (Fig 2). Consequently, although the medieval waterfront has been lost along much of the east bank of the Witham, remnants may be found further inland in some areas.

Trade and governance

Water was responsible for Boston's development as a port, and the trade that accompanied this allowed the town to grow and to flourish. Boston's location, just inland from the east coast, made it an attractive base for fishing fleets and also attracted much continental trade. Strong trade links with the Baltic culminated in Boston becoming a Hanseatic port – the Hansa merchants established their own guildhouse (known as the steelyard) and warehouses in, or just outside, the town, and were a crucial source of revenue for Boston. The high number of European immigrants influenced the development of the town, notably in encouraging the early adoption of brick: an early 14th-century brickyard was discovered in Boston, suggesting the importation of skills as well as materials.[13]

Boston's mercantile trade was focused on the east side of the River Witham in the Fee of Richmond, where the Market Place still stands, but is thought to have expanded into the Fee of Creoun on the west side of the river as early as the late 12th century. By the time of Gough's map in *c* 1375 (*see* p 4) Boston

Figure 2
An aerial view of Boston, looking north-west, taken in 1930, showing the straightening of the River Witham beyond St Botolph's Church.
[EPW031902]

is clearly shown as straddling the River Witham and although the first documentary record of a town bridge dates to 1305[14] it is likely that a crossing existed previously.

Much of the early trade was in wool which was sent from Lincoln via the Witham to Boston and onwards to the Low Countries. Consequently, by 1204, Boston's port trade was second only to London in value and duty revenue raised.[15] A mark of Boston's increasing mercantile importance came in 1369 when Boston was made one of only 11 Staple towns for wool nationally[16] (at the expense of Lincoln which had been awarded the Staple only 16 years previously). The award of the Staple meant that all wool within the region, Lincolnshire, Nottinghamshire, Leicestershire and Derbyshire – an area rich in religious holdings involved in the production of wool – had to be sent to Boston to be weighed and sealed before it could be traded onwards. Such a stipulation clearly brought with it significant economic advantages to a port town such as Boston.

Boston benefited from weekly markets, but most famously from its fair. The earliest reference to the fair is a charter from 1125, granting trading rights at Boston fair to the Abbey of St Mary in York,[17] and by 1172 £67 and 18d from the 'fair of Holland' was paid to the Treasury by Count Conan, Earl of Richmond.[18] St Botolph's fair, held in the Market Place each summer, was not only nationally important (the Court of Hustings in London suspending its sittings for the duration of the fair and the kings' tailor and falconer attending frequently) but also internationally, thanks to the presence of foreign traders.[19]

Boston's guilds were hugely influential, wealthy and powerful organisations that were concerned both with religion and trade – many securing papal privileges for members, such as the right to bestow indulgences of pardon, in exchange for a fee. Fourteen religious guilds were founded from the 13th century onwards, the most important being the guilds of St Mary, Corpus Christi, St Peter and St Paul, Holy Trinity and St George. These five guilds were subject to royal licence and were known to have guildhalls and property within Boston – St Mary, St Peter and St Paul and Corpus Christi also having chapels within St Botolph's Church. St Mary's guild chapel occupied a prestigious location at the east end of the south aisle, close to the altar, whilst the guild of St Peter and St Paul had the east end of the north aisle and the chapel of Corpus Christi was attached to the outside of the church.[20] Three guildhalls are known to have been demolished – those of Holy Trinity on Gascoyne Row, Wormgate; St Peter and

St Paul in Wide Bargate; and St George near St George's Lane. Two guildhalls do, however, survive – most notably that of St Mary on South Street, and, more tentatively, the guildhall of Corpus Christi which is thought to have been in Shodfriars Hall (*see* Fig 11)[21]

A church has occupied the site of St Botolph's since at least the 12th century but the present building (Fig 3) dates largely from the 14th century and, despite the economic decline at the time, is testament to the continued wealth of Boston's citizens. The first phase of the current church was constructed from stone between 1309 and 1390 to replace an earlier wooden church and is essentially a monument to Boston's merchants. The vast nave, famous tower and inclusion of guild chapels put the design emphasis firmly on those areas used by the laity, the chancel itself being comparatively small. Beyond St Botolph's, Boston was prosperous enough to support numerous other religious foundations, including a hospital and four friaries. Boston also attracted investment from a number of abbeys which are known to have held land in the town – notably Fountains Abbey, which held land adjoining Wormgate and gave its name to Fountain Lane.

Most religious holdings were concentrated on the east side of the river, but the Carmelites had a friary in the vicinity of West Street, built in 1307 and extended in 1350.[22] The exact location and extent of their holdings remains uncertain, but a series of excavations at Paddock Grove and on the High Street have found substantial ashlar walls and deposits of blocks dating from the 13th or 14th century.[23] Blackfriars Arts Centre on Spain Lane (named for the de Spayne family) is believed to have been the refectory range of the Dominican friary (Fig 4), whilst part of the 1309 church was incorporated into No 10 South Street. The Dominican friars built a conduit to bring water from Bolingbroke, more than 20 miles away, to their friary and the town, suggesting that fresh drinking water was hard to obtain within and around Boston.

Boston suffered a series of fires throughout the 13th century – in 1281, in 1288, when Robert Chamberlain was hanged for arson[24] following the destruction of much of the town, and also in 1290.[25] Archaeological evidence to support this was found during an excavation at South Square.[26] Boston's economic strength allowed it to recover from the immediate aftermath of such devastation, but the start of the 14th century heralded a period of decline due in large part to the contraction of the wool trade. No doubt recurrent episodes of

Figure 3
The famous tower of St Botolph's Church, fondly known as 'the Stump', was built between c 1450 and 1520 but the chancel, nave and aisles were built between 1309 and 1390.
[CC98/00001]

Figure 4
The Blackfriars Arts Centre on Spain Lane is believed
to have been the refectory range of the 14th-century
Dominican friary.
[DP161495]

the plague, combined with periodic flooding and the silting of the Fossdyke and the River Witham, contributed to the economic woes which continued to worsen throughout the 15th and 16th centuries, at which time only 200 sacks of wool and 100 cloths passed through the port each year (compared to 3,000 of each even in the late 14th century).[27] In 1563 Boston had only 471 recorded households, perhaps 2,000 residents – less than half the *c* 5,700 recorded in the 1377 poll tax return.[28]

Morphology

The Reformation resulted in the dissolution of all the guilds and religious houses and the creation of the Borough of Boston in 1545. A new Corporation was formed to assume responsibility for the administration of the town and market and was comprised largely of leading members of the old guilds. By this time, however, the influence of water, trade and religion had already helped to form the streetscape of Boston which, by and large, is still visible today. The east side of the Market Place is divided into groups of buildings by narrow passageways and lanes. In the medieval period these marked the edges of burgage plots, or groups of burgage plots which were known as 'curia'. Each burgage plot within a curia was narrow but long, allowing for a row of buildings to be built stretching east towards the Barditch and accessed by a lane.

Wide Bargate

Still in partial use as a market today, Wide Bargate appears to be the fossilisation of a medieval market place to the north of the main market, with references as early as c 1200 mentioning the horse market (and houses) 'beyond the Bar'.[29] The rectilinear Market Place, surrounded by radiating narrow alleys, is typical of a planned and controlled market and the continuing influence of the Church and the Earl of Richmond allowed this large area to be kept free from encroaching buildings as the town expanded. The market place in Bargate to the north is again typical in both form and location for a secondary, later, market – situated on the edge of the town, connected by a 'gate', it is triangular or funnel-shaped in plan. Funnnel-shaped market places are generally associated with livestock markets and were well-established as the basic form of markets in Europe, for example at Halle, Aachen, Soest and Bonn.[30]

Wormgate

Situated to the north of St Botolph's Church and occupying the highest ground in Boston, it is one of Boston's oldest streets. Excavation has revealed the remains of walls dating to around the 12th century, replaced by a 14th-century building and, in turn, by a 17th-century building which was demolished in the 1960s.[31] Wormgate was known as Deppol or Deep-Pool Gate (where the Barditch joined the river) into the 16th century. It is thought that the name Wormgate comes from Wymegate – Wyme itself being a version of Witham. Again, the plots along Wormgate are fairly regular in size, suggesting that the street was deliberately planned.[32]

South Street and South Square

To the south of the main Market Place, another remnant of the medieval town, late 12th-century artefacts were found during excavations at South Square,[33] suggesting that medieval Boston was focused on the east side of the River Witham and immediately surrounding the market. The guildhalls of St Mary and Corpus Christi are known to have had associated quays but no archaeological evidence for these has been found along the present waterfront. As with Wormgate the course of South Street suggests that it once paralleled the river and that the bend of the river has been pushed out since, meaning the old waterfront is now buried inland.

Extant examples

Extant examples of Boston's early buildings are not numerous, although fragments are known to survive within buildings which have been substantially altered in later years. Such fragments are important and there are likely to be a number of buildings containing as-yet unidentified early fabric which may be able to tell us more about the history and development of the town. One of the best known and complete of Boston's early buildings is surely the Grade I listed St Mary's Guildhall on South Street (Fig 5). Built *c* 1390 around the time of the guild's incorporation, the Guildhall is one of the oldest post-Roman brick structures in England, built using bricks and tiles produced locally.[34] St Mary's Guildhall is similar in form and function to Trinity Hall in York, built by a fraternity between 1356 and 1367, and itself influenced other guildhalls including the Holy Trinity (1421) and St George's (early–mid-15th century) guildhalls in nearby King's Lynn.[35] The exact internal arrangement of rooms and their functions is still somewhat unclear but the chapel is believed to have been located on the ground floor at the western end, with a ceremonial entrance from the street. Beyond the chapel were stores or accommodation for bedesmen (the arrangement of blocked doors and windows suggests room for six or seven cells).[36] The position of the current 18th-century doorway near the centre of the southern elevation is the most likely position for the original main entrance[37] and documentary records suggest that the land to the south (where Fydell House now stands) was formerly open with a series of high-status oriel windows

Figure 5
St Mary's Guildhall, South Street, built c *1390. The narrow gable wall of the Guildhall, enhanced by a vast traceried window, is the result of the constricted burgage plots of the medieval period.*
[DP161491]

to the south elevation of the building.[38] The gaol cells on the ground floor were inserted *c* 1552 when the Guildhall became the home of the Boston Corporation and are said to have briefly held members of the Pilgrim Fathers who attempted to sail from Boston to Holland in 1607 but were captured and tried at the Guildhall.[39] Subsequent Puritan migrants were, of course, more successful and included many Boston residents (including the vicar, John Cotton, in 1633), resulting in the founding of Boston, Massachusetts. The upper floor of St Mary's Guildhall consisted of a hall over the chapel, with a dais and traceried window at the west end and chambers and services beyond to the east. The west window is stylistically similar to one at the Collegiate Church of All Saints, Maidstone, dated 1395 and attributed to the Master Mason Henry Yeveley.[40] The courtroom beyond the hall, which connects to the cells below, was also put in *c* 1552 (Fig 6).[41]

St Mary's Guildhall is the earliest use of brick construction in Boston but the Grade II* listed Hussey Tower[42], approximately one quarter of a mile to the south-east, is an important example in its own right (Fig 7). The tower is believed to have originated in the late 15th century as a detached solar tower which would have served a separate hall.[43] The Hussey Tower is, at first glance, in an odd location: to the south of the medieval market town and set far back from the river. It has been suggested that the Hansa steelyard may have been located in this area, possibly hinting at a mercantile base away from the town centre. Merchants' houses with towers are not unknown in the region and comparisons have been made to Rochford Tower in Skirbeck, a tower house of *c* 1510. However, examples like Clifton House in King's Lynn (Fig 8), with its five-storey brick tower of *c* 1570 located close to the wharf, are clearly more developed designs which dominate their immediate surroundings.

Remains of the Dominican friary (Blackfriars) lie within several buildings on South Street. Most notably, No 10 South Street (which is Grade II* listed), contains within its basement a substantial section of what is postulated to be a cloister arcade and vaulted undercroft associated with the *c* 1309 church (Fig 9). Although the façade to South Street is a 19th-century design, a 14th-century blocked doorway at ground level on the north elevation hints at what lies behind (Fig 10). Adjoining is No 12 South Street, the 18th-century Custom House. Within the yard to the rear is an arcade which is believed to be a continuation of that seen at No 10.

Figure 6
*The front rooms of the Guildhall, not seen here,
consisted of a hall above a chapel. The rooms beyond
are the result of a series of alterations, with
16th-century cells below a courtroom, fine Georgian
panelled rooms and a substantial kitchen.*

Shodfriars Hall on South Street, Grade II* listed, is one of Boston's only buildings to have extensive timber-framing clearly visible (Fig 11). Built in the early 15th century the building has been tentatively identified as the guildhall of Corpus Christi, but the present day layout is largely the result of a restoration by

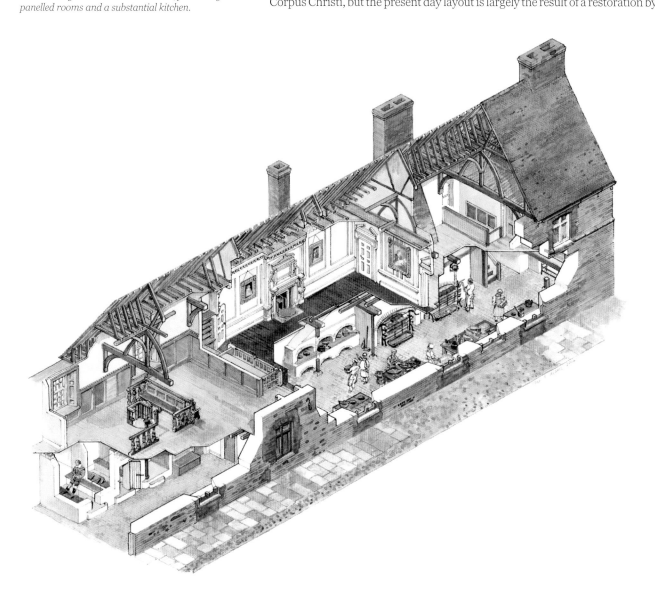

George Gilbert Scott Jnr and his brother John Oldrid Scott in the 1870s. The restoration and extension of the building to its present extent resulted in many timbers being added to the façade, and some original timbers moved (Fig 12). But more of the façade is original than might perhaps be expected.

Tucked away beside the river to the south of St Botolph's is No 30 Church Street, a modest building with exposed timber-framing (Fig 13). Carpenters' marks suggest that two bays have been lost to the south and the building has clearly been much altered over the years. However, enough of the structure remains to suggest that it may be a 16th-century remnant of one of the rows which once radiated from the Market Place.

Pescod Hall, situated in Pescod Square, was built *c* 1450 and was originally much larger. It was approached along Mitre Lane and it appears that part of an associated structure, possibly a gatehouse, straddled the lane until the early 19th century.[44] The remains of the hall were dismantled and re-erected close to its current location in 1974 after being moved to make way for commercial development. The building was moved to its present location in 2003, again to make way for commercial development, but a timber survey carried out in 2001 shows that, during this latest move, the building was rotated by 180 degrees. The survey also revealed how few of the timbers are original – the south-east comer (as it presently stands) is the only section with any substantial quantity of primary fabric (Fig 14).[45]

A number of the buildings around the Market Place appear, at first sight, to be 18th century or later in date, but contain fascinating remnants of timber-framed buildings. In many cases the best clue to the origin of the building is the steep pitch of the roofline. No 27–8 Market Place was a 15th-century jettied building with 18th-century alterations which was re-fronted in the 19th century and then significantly altered in the 1980s when the first-floor timber-framing to the rear of the building was removed. Similarly Nos 19 and 24 Market Place retain 15th-century fabric largely hidden by 18th- and 19th-century alterations.

Nos 25 and 35 High Street, to the west of the river, are 15th-century hall houses where the hall, fronted by a shop, lies perpendicular to the street (Figs 15, 16 and 17). Although partially re-fronted and rebuilt, substantial quantities of original timber-framing remain. A number of other 15th- or 16th-century timber-framed buildings are known or suspected to survive further south on the

Figure 7 (opposite, top)
The Hussey Tower, off Skirbeck Road, was built in the
late 15th century as part of a complex of buildings and
would have served as a solar tower for a detached hall.
[DP161450]

Figure 8 (opposite, bottom)
Clifton House, King's Lynn, Norfolk, is a merchant's
tower house of c 1570. Built perhaps 100 years later
than the Hussey Tower, Clifton House is clearly more
elaborate in form, height and decoration but reflects the
same desire to impress.
[BB92/19423]

Figure 9 (right)
The remains of a possible cloister arcade with carved
corbels have been incorporated within No 10 South
Street and are believed to be part of the c 1309 church
of the Dominican friary.
[AA44/09297]

Figure 10 (below)
A 14th-century doorway visible on the north elevation
of No 10 South Street. The wall itself contains some
large ashlar blocks.
[John Minnis]

Figure 11 (right)
Shodfriars Hall, as seen from South Street. The early 15th-century timber-framed building has been tentatively (based on a documentary reference and comparison with Thaxted guildhall in Essex) identified as the guildhall of Corpus Christi.
[DP161484]

Figure 12 (below)
This photograph of Shodfriars Hall prior to the restoration work by the Scotts in the 1870s illustrates the extent of the work carried out, but a substantial number of original timbers did survive – particularly on the ground floor.
[AL0232/027/02]

Figure 13 (below, right)
No 30 Church Street may be a remaining fragment of one of the many rows of buildings which once radiated from the Market Place.
[John Minnis]

High Street – including Nos 82[46] and 93 (Fig 18) suggesting that by the end of the 16th century Boston had expanded well beyond its earlier limits.

Boston's Grammar School, located off South Street, moved from Wormgate to its current home in 1567. This is a single-storey red-brick building with a central bay window and stone detailing. To the northern end of the Market Place

Figure 14
Pescod Hall is remarkable for having been much reduced, altered and moved several times – most recently in 2003 – but some original timbers of the c 1450 building remain.
[John Minnis]

Figure 15
No 25 High Street. Located on the west side of the river this 15th-century jettied hall house is easily overlooked.
[John Minnis]

are a number of buildings with 17th-century origins, including Nos 3–4a Petticoat Lane (No 3 distinguished by its green-tiled roof) which has a date stone from the 1660s in the east gable wall – since obscured by later developments. No 57–8 Market Place (Fig 19) is a mid-17th century building complete with reset wainscotting to one of the second-floor rooms. To the north of St Botolph's, Church House on the corner of Wormgate is a charming brick building of the mid-17th century (Fig 20). Built in the Artisan Mannerist style, it has a shaped gable and decorative brick bands.

Boston today is a town shaped by its past as a nationally and internationally important port and centre for trade. The very early history of Boston is not well understood at present, in no small part due to the complications of deep excavations in a waterlogged area, and it is hoped that further work in the area will answer questions regarding the earliest permanent settlement and the extent of the early town. During its medieval heyday Boston attracted investment from religious orders and private merchants who invested heavily in buildings, some of which may still be seen today. Sadly many of Boston's great buildings have been lost due to fires, floods and the passing of time but the street pattern we see today in the town centre is remarkable in having changed little over the past 700 years.

Figure 16 (above)
No 35 High Street is another 15th-century hall house. Although restored in recent years a number of early timbers are visible in the southern gable wall. [DP165415]

Figure 17 (left)
A view down the side of No 35 High Street, looking from the rear of the property towards the street, showing timber-framing with brick infill panels. [John Minnis]

Figure 18 (above)
No 93 High Street, one of a number of 16th-century buildings known to survive on the High Street.
[John Minnis]

Figure 19 (above, left)
The somewhat unprepossessing No 57–8 Market Place, a mid-17th century building complete with wainscotting.
[John Minnis]

Figure 20 (left)
Church House, Wormgate – an unusual brick building of the mid-17th century designed in what is sometimes referred to as the 'Fen Artisan Mannerist' style.
[DP165490]

A PLAN
Of the Borough & Port
OF
Boston,
In the County of Lincoln.
Survey'd in the Year 1741.
BY
Robert Hall

Maud Foster's Drain

Explanation.
Hammonbeck
St Anns Lane
Talbercroft Lane
White Horse Lane
Water Lane
Donghky Key
Water Lane
Emery Lane
Rainbow Lane
Lawrence Lane
Spoonmakers Lane
Gunfold Lane
St Georges Hall
Lincoln Lane
St Boltolphs Hall
Butcher Row
Thatchers Row Lane
Angel Lane
Fountain Lane
Church Lane
Petticoat Lane
Meal Yard
Sheep Pens
Mill Hill
Part of Skirbeck
St Peters Lane
Corpus Christi Lane
Thieves Lane
Seed Lane
Tatter Lane
Dolphin Lane
The Pumps
Brown Yard
Rockbarn Lane
Mill Lane
Grants Lane
Peacock Lane
Hawthorn Lane
Posey Lane
Red Lyon Lane
Custom House Lane

Bardiche

Bardiche

Bardiche

Bardiche

South End

Goat Street, or High Street

THE RIVER WITHAM

Fenthorn Lane

Skirbe

To Freiston

Segill Mostle

To the Reverend
Bernard Wilson DD
of Westheal in the County of
Lincoln Prebendary of Worcester
This PLAN

2
18th-century Boston

In the earlier part of the 18th century, Boston's overseas trade had stagnated to the point where it had been overtaken by King's Lynn as the principal port on the Wash. However, despite the Haven continuing to silt up, it retained a substantial coastal trade. Steps were taken to provide better drainage of the surrounding fens with the North and South Forty-Foot Drains being dug in *c* 1720 and the 1760s respectively, but the real need was to improve the Witham Navigation and drain the land adjacent to it. After several plans were proposed, the work of widening and straightening the river at its southern end was authorised in 1762 and completed in 1766 with the construction of the Grand Sluice. Some years earlier, in 1742, the Town Bridge linking the two halves of the town had been reconstructed.

Changes in agriculture following Enclosure Acts in the parishes to the west and north of Boston, and further improvements to the River Witham at the upper reaches, led to a great improvement in the fortunes of the town. Boston's prosperity in this period is evident from the large number of new houses put up for some of its more prominent citizens and, in the final quarter of the century, with the Corporation itself embarking on a building programme. Our detailed knowledge of the town's topography begins in this period with the publication in 1741 of the first street plan of Boston by Robert Hall (*opposite*).

Housing the well-to-do

Unlike other Lincolnshire towns such as Stamford or Grantham, Boston was not dominated by a single aristocratic family living nearby. It was represented in Parliament for much of the century by the Bertie family but they lived a considerable distance away. Like all provincial towns not dominated by nearby aristocratic landlords, Boston had a number of wealthy and influential local families who derived their income from trade and banking and this had architectural implications.

The most splendid of Boston's 18th-century houses is also one of the earliest to survive, Fydell House (Fig 21), in South Square, is believed to have been designed early in the century by William Sands of Spalding for the Jackson family and derives its name from Joseph Fydell who acquired it in 1726.[47] The Fydells were merchants who had extensive property interests in the town and

Robert Hall's plan of Boston 1741, the earliest plan of the town. [Reproduced with permission from Richard Kay Publications, originally reproduced by Richard Kay Publications in 1974]

Figure 21
Fydell House, South Square, a fine early 18th century house, that was saved by a pioneering building trust.
[DP161482]

Figure 22
No 116 High Street showing the house as restored in 2010. The three-storey house to its left, built in the early 19th century, was also owned by the Garfits and formed part of their bank.
[DP160254]

Figure 23 (above)
The Ionic doorway of No 120 High Street.
[DP161441]

Figure 24 (above, right)
The imposing façade of No 120 High Street, flanked by its later wings.
[DP161440]

dominated local politics until the middle of the 19th century. Fydell House displays very high-quality materials and craftsmanship throughout. Internally, the fittings reflect the status of the house with extensive panelling on the ground floor with fluted Doric pilasters and a good staircase with a mixture of fluted, plain and twisted balusters and pretty rococo plasterwork on the walls.

No 116 High Street (Fig 22) was built for William Garfit II, probably in 1728. He opened the first private bank in Lincolnshire in 1754 which remained in these premises until 1864, and his descendants lived here until 1891. A five-bay, two-storey house with a handsome fanlight, it was extensively modified in 1882 with a new staircase in a neo-Jacobean style by William Henry Wheeler. Following a long period of decay, it has recently been restored for community use (*see* p 108).

A few doors to the south, No 120 High Street dates from the second half of the 18th century and is much grander with three storeys and a projecting pedimented central section (Figs 23 and 24). Flanking wings with canted

Figure 25
Tunnard House, 20 Wide Bargate is a stately town mansion of the late 18th century, its sole ornament being the fine Doric doorcase.
[DP165421]

Figure 26
Although much smaller, Samuel Tunnard's business premises next to his house were more ornate with broad fanlights over the ground floor windows giving a good deal of light to the offices.
[DP165420]

façades were added later, probably in the early 19th century. The pediment bears a striking cartouche with a rabbit's head, which suggests a connection with the local Tunnard family who used 'Coney' as a first name. By 1826, the house was occupied by the Claypon banking family. With the decline in status of the area, it was acquired in the early 1900s by Frederick Palmer, then the largest ratepayer in the town, who developed its garden, which formerly extended to the river, with terraces of houses forming Oxford Street. Another house of considerable ambition is Tunnard House, No 20 Wide Bargate, which has a wide frontage and a handsome Doric doorcase (Fig 25). A E Richardson said that as 'pure architecture ... it was beyond compeer [sic]'[48]. It was built for the lawyer Samuel Tunnard about 1790, together with his offices next door at No 22 with particularly elegant segmental-headed windows which incorporate broad fanlights (Fig 26). No 20 was extended at the rear in the 1960s and lost much of its interior in subsequent uses which have included a spell as the Boston County Club and currently as a restaurant.

Housing for the middle class

Many residents occupied substantial terraced properties such as Nos 43–57, High Street. No 49 reflects the maritime interests of one of its former owners in having ships painted in the overmantels of its fireplaces (Fig 27). This is a feature found in other coastal towns, such as Berwick-upon-Tweed. Today, the part of London Road facing the river is something of a backwater since it was bypassed with the opening of Spalding Road. It was once, together with the southern part of the High Street, the principal entrance to the town from the south and heavily built up. Existing timber-framed buildings, such as No 93 High Street had new rendered façades applied to modernise them and much new building took place, partly to replace existing structures but also on new sites, extending the town's built-up area. One of the earliest to be built, if the date of 1718 on its downpipe hopper can be believed, was No 107 High Street, a three-storey house, modest in scale but with a fine doorcase and fanlight (Fig 28). Of similar date is the group of four houses at Nos 119–125 High Street, each with three-light windows like ones seen in Pump Square (*see* Fig 32). Other new work included pubs such as the Ship Inn and the large former Crown and Anchor inn, built about 1803 and

Figure 27
The interior of No 49 High Street in April 1944, showing the painted overmantel on the first floor, depicting seafaring subjects.
[AA44/09293]

closed as an inn about 1860, warehouses, serving the quay opposite, and fashionable houses such as Nos 2–3 London Road (Fig 29).

Perhaps the most intriguing of these new buildings is the group at Nos 124–136 High Street, which forms a row of seven houses. Despite the best efforts of historians over the years, it has proved impossible to discover the origins of this remarkable terrace which is known locally as 'The Barracks' (Fig 30). There is, however, no evidence to indicate a military purpose. The most likely explanation is that it was built as a warehouse, probably in the first half of the 18th century (it is shown on Hall's plan of 1741(*see* p 22), hence the continuous roofline, the division into 18 narrow bays and the generally massive appearance. The aesthetic is undeniably industrial rather than domestic and the doors and windows would appear to have been added in the early 19th century on conversion to houses.

One of the first planned developments beyond the Barditch to the east was Pump Square, marked on Hall's map as The Pumps. It was built up in the mid- to late 18th century with elegant three-storey red-brick houses. The earliest, Nos 1–2 on the north side (originally a terrace of three houses) and Nos 7–10 on the east side have hipped roofs and elegant dentilled eaves seen elsewhere in Boston

Figure 28 (above)
Photographed on 5 June 1942, No 107 High Street has changed very little in appearance since then.
[OP19515]

Figure 29 (left)
The late 18th-century houses on London Road exemplify the way in which Boston grew along the main road out of the town to the south. Nos 2–3 (on the right) contrast with the later No 4 Ferry House (formerly Marine House) with its stuccoed façade. The proximity of the Haven is evident with the houses punctuated by large warehouses.
[John Minnis]

(Figs 31 and 32). Nos 1–2 have broad three-light windows while Nos 7–10 only have them on the ground floors. Around the end of the 19th century, Nos 7–10 were fitted with elaborate brick doorcases in an attempt to make them look more modern. The windows of these houses have their frames set almost flush with the brickwork, pointing to their earlier date. They contrast with Nos 5–6 in the north-east corner of the square which were added later and have recessed window frames, stone rather than brick lintels, and timber doorcases similar in design to those in Witham Place (*see* Fig 37). These houses were probably built at the same time as a group in Main Ridge East, around the corner to the east.

Figure 30
The extraordinary block known locally as 'The Barracks', restored by the Boston Preservation Trust, is probably of industrial rather than military origin.
[DP161443]

Figure 31
The northern end of Pump Square with Nos 1–2, of similar date to Nos 7–10, on the left and the later Nos 5–6, with their recessed sash windows on the right. [DP161470]

Figure 32 (left)
Nos 7–10 Pump Square with dentilled eaves and almost flush sash windows of the mid-18th century. The late 19th-century door surrounds add an incongruous note. [DP161468]

Figure 33 (opposite, top)
With its warm red-brick walls and pantiled roof, No 16 Wormgate is typical of smaller Boston houses built during the 18th century. Although of simple design, a well-proportioned timber doorcase and a sympathetic shopfront of recent origin do much to enhance its appearance. [DP165025]

Figure 34 (opposite, bottom)
Wormgate preserves much of the appearance of 18th-century Boston with small buildings on either side of a narrow street, many of 18th-century or earlier origin. [DP161174]

Pump Square was approached from the Market Place by no fewer than three medieval streets: Dolphin Lane, Still Lane and Grants Lane. Dolphin Lane, slightly wider than the other two, became a popular shopping street and most of the present buildings along it date from the early 19th century. But at the time the houses in Pump Square were constructed, they stood, as was common in most towns, almost cheek by jowl with a mixture of small cottages and warehouses. Boston's poor were housed in timber-framed medieval houses and brick cottages from the 17th and 18th centuries that have almost completely disappeared. Those that survived into the 20th century were mainly centred around Fountain Lane, off Wormgate (Figs 33 and 34) and in the Rosegarth Street/Pinfold Lane area on the west bank of the Witham and were demolished in slum clearance programmes.

Public provision

Like many authorities, Boston Corporation derived an income from tolls and harbour dues but it also, unusually, had a substantial estate of its own, formed from the lands of the guild of St Mary, which by 1837 was worth £2,137 pa. These lands, known as the Erection Lands, provided around £1,380 pa after deductions for salaries and charities, much of which was spent on public works.

In 1769, the Corporation decided to build a new Fish Market but by the time construction began, the decision had been taken to incorporate it in a terrace of houses. The architect was Thomas Lumby of Lincoln, best known for early Gothic Revival work at Lincoln Cathedral and at Doddington church.[49] The terrace, completed in 1770 in fashionable white gault brick, is dominated by its central pediment and has the appearance of a palace (*see* Fig 102). The rear elevation, which was clearly visible from the Town Bridge, was treated with the same degree of architectural finish as the front, although subsequent additions have detracted from this. Corporation Buildings is one of the earliest publicly funded housing developments in England, although the prosperous merchants for whom the houses were intended were a far cry from the tenants of social housing today.

3

The expansion of Boston 1790–1860

Until the late 18th century, Boston had remained largely within the bounds of the medieval town. It encompassed the area bounded by the Barditch to the east and the north, a small built-up area on the west side of the River Witham centred on the High Street, and southwards to London Road and the Grammar School. Only Wide Bargate and some development along the Maud Foster Drain north of Bargate Bridge extended beyond the medieval core.

From the 1790s Boston saw significant expansion, following the draining of Holland Fen in the 1760s and the East, West and Wildmore Fens, completed in 1813, which led to it becoming the principal port for transporting the greatly increased arable production of the area. Prosperity returned to the town which had six banks active between 1805 and 1814, more than any other town in Lincolnshire. By this time it was again the leading commercial and industrial town in the county – and the richest. Its population rose from 6,465 in 1801 to 11,637 in 1821. Substantial development occurred along the principal roads leading out of the town and several entirely new residential areas sprang up to meet demand for housing. In the first half of the 19th century, Boston had become the largest town in Lincolnshire, with a population of 17,561 by 1851.

This rising prosperity was reflected in improvements to the town with street lighting being introduced in 1776, followed by the setting up of an Improvement Commission in 1796. This saw new streets created, such as Bridge Street (Fig 35), with its handsome terrace of shops on the north side, and New Street, giving access to new developments north of Wormgate.

The timber bridge of 1742 was proving inadequate and John Rennie, as the engineer for the 1800 drainage of the fens immediately to the north of Boston, was asked by the Boston Corporation to advise on its replacement. Rennie, who rivalled Thomas Telford as the greatest bridge builder of his generation, prepared four designs later that year, two in stone and two in iron. While stone was more durable, a bridge of iron was cheaper and quicker to build. The Corporation decided on iron construction and Rennie went ahead with what was his first iron bridge, completed in 1807. It was replaced by the present Town Bridge in 1913. In 1812, an Act for the Improvement of the Port led to the rebuilding of the banks of the Haven in brick with stone edgings, still to be seen on South Street Quay today. The work was overseen by Rennie, who also carried out work on Maud Foster Drain, building a new sluice where it entered the River Witham.

John Wood's plan of Boston, 1829.
[Reproduced with permission from Richard Kay Publications, originally reproduced by Richard Kay Publications in 1993]

North of the centre

Wormgate marked the northern exit from the medieval town and, from the late 1790s, building took place to its north on Witham Place and on the land behind it, creating a new suburb beyond the medieval streets clustered to the east of Wormgate. The first of the houses to go up were Nos 1–10, Witham Place built as a speculation between 1795 and 1799 by John Watson, related by marriage to Jeptha Pacey (*see* p 91). These, because they were some of the first houses in Boston to be given numbers, were known by the somewhat unprepossessing name of the 'number slabs'. They were of red brick, three storeys high, and the ground-floor windows were not aligned with those above. The roofs, partly hidden behind parapets, are pantiled like most older buildings in Boston. Today, most of the houses have plate-glass sash windows with margin lights, replacing the original multi-pane sashes at some point in the 19th century (Fig 36).

Although the elevations of the houses are quite plain in appearance, what stands out are the delightfully varied doorcases (Fig 37). Nos 2–3 have a full pediment with much enrichment including a Greek key band above the door, No 7 has a Doric doorcase with metopes and guttae and a much deeper rectangular fanlight with glazing bars of decidedly rococo form, while No 9 combines this with a heavily dentilled pediment. No 12 is different again, with a chunky bolection moulding and a canopy on shaped brackets. Some of these are likely to be later replacements or modifications but the overall effect is attractive. No 14 is a large house with a fanlight of spider's-web type. Windows on the sides away from the façade were smaller; a survivor is a small Yorkshire sliding sash high in the gable of No 3. Several of the houses were occupied as schools from an early date, evidently of a genteel kind. In 1803, the occupant of No 6 advertised as follows: 'Her house which is neatly and genteely fitted up, being in such an open, airy and healthy Part of the town, she flatters herself it will be found a very eligible situation as a Boarding house for those young Ladies whose Friends may wish them to enjoy the Benefits of being constantly under her care and Attention ... .'[50]

On the earlier part of Wormgate to the south of Witham Place, many of its buildings were given new shopfronts in the early 19th century, some incorporating reeding and bowed fascias as at Nos 19 and 27 on the east side and No 10 on the west side. Other shops in the street have excellent shopfronts from later on in the century. Indeed, historic shopfronts are one of the things

Figure 35
The north side of Bridge Street, opened early in the 19th century at the instigation of the Boston Improvement Commissioners, retains many of its original buildings. [DP161386]

Figure 36
Nos 6–10 Witham Place built by John Watson between
1795 and 1799.
[John Minnis]

that make Boston stand out, with other early examples in Dolphin Lane and in the Market Place where Nos 27–8 retain a bowed window.

The streets to the east – Red Lion Street, Witham Street, Chapel Street and Union Place – were of inferior status and the houses built there were much smaller than those of Witham Place, mainly of two storeys and on small plots with little more than backyards, rather than gardens. These streets were developed somewhat later than Witham Place but most of the houses were there by 1819. Unlike Witham Place, which was listed in 1949, very few of the houses in these streets have been listed, although they are in a conservation area. Consequently, most have undergone extensive changes to doors and windows in the last 30 years which have removed many of the characteristic details that would help to date them. Some of the developments are of medium size: the north side of Red Lion Street is relatively uniform with a row of seven fairly substantial terraced houses, each with a rounded fanlight (Nos 33–45), then a group of four much smaller houses (Nos 17–23), again the work of a single

builder, employing white facing bricks and timber doorcases of a type widely found in Boston. By contrast, the houses on the south side of the street are a textbook example of small-scale development on single plots by individual builders over a period of time. Nos 26–30 are three-storied but much smaller than those in Witham Place. Two of them are by the same builder, with bands below the first- and second-floor windows, and they contrast with the third which is much lower in height. The remaining houses vary greatly in height with two of them much later infill or replacements of earlier properties.

The southern part of Red Lion Street is completely different in character from that running due west and was at first envisaged as one side of a square but the other three sides were not built, apart from a theatre, erected in 1806 (demolished). Centenary Methodist Church was later built on what would have been the garden in the centre of the square. The buildings, which date from *c* 1808, are much larger than those in the western part of the street. They include two substantial houses: No 7 has a handsome reeded doorcase with guttae and metopes and a fanlight with margin glazing, together with its original door (*see* those in Pen Street). This part of the street ceased to be residential in the mid-19th century and most of the houses acquired shopfronts, some good late 19th-century examples remaining.

A similar mix of houses is to be seen in Chapel Street, all but one being of two storeys. No 5 retains one of the distinctive timber doorcases of typical Regency design (circular motif in square in top corners and recessed panels with convex ends in the pilasters and door over panel) found throughout much of Boston in the early 19th century. Witham Street and Union Place offer more variety. Nos 10–14 Witham Street seem to be the oldest houses in the area with a steeply pitched pantile roof and attic rooms, lit by a small window in the end gable in the case of No 14. Their windows appear to have been tripartite with segmental heads, something shared with No 1, which has windows of such a large size that it might suggest it was built with a business use in mind. Union Place has one much larger house, No 2, with a doorcase similar to that at No 5 Chapel Street and two further houses (Nos 12 and 14) have similar doorcases but with reeding to the pilasters.

Social provision for this new quarter included a number of public houses. The Carpenters Arms in Witham Street, a substantial three-storey red-brick building, survives in use and retains much of its character. Although many of the

Figure 37 (clockwise from top left)
No 2 Witham Place; No 7 Witham Place; No 23 Pen Street; No 44 Witham Bank West; No 7 Red Lion Street; No 37 Pen Street; The Presbytery, Horncastle Road; No 2 Grove Street.
[John Minnis; John Minnis; DP161465; DP151446; DP161476; DP161467; DP161448; John Minnis]

streets to the north of Red Lion Street were narrow, the variety of housing provision suggests a wide cross section of people lived in the area. It was a definite step above the teeming alleys that ran off the Market Place or the tenements of the Lincoln Lane area.

Witham Town and the surrounding area

The opening of the Witham Navigation in 1766 led to considerable industrial development along the riverside north of the existing built-up area and formed the first substantial expansion of Boston since medieval times. A large new warehouse with a steeply pitched roof (still extant) was constructed soon after. Further north, facing the newly straightened River Witham, William Howden established a substantial iron foundry. In the early 19th century he built Witham Bank House and its neighbour, which is a tour de force in ornamental ironwork with porch, gate and railings all exhibiting originality and fine workmanship and acting as an advertisement for its owner's products (Figs 38 and 39).

Many other businesses connected with wharfage and handling goods created a demand for labour. Passenger traffic along the Witham was served by an enormous inn, the Barge Inn (Fig 40). The building had a low pitched hipped roof with broad eaves supported on paired brackets but its most distinctive features were the segmental arches with wave-moulded keystones over the windows, some of which had glazed fanlights. These arches were another distinctive Boston detail of the period: they are to be seen in the Unitarian Chapel (1819) (*see* Fig 53) and houses built along Windsor Bank (*see* Fig 48) at the same time.

Housing was required for the employees of the industries springing up in the area. It took the form of a number of streets off Tattershall Road, including Witham Green, which had a number of short streets running off it, and Reform Place. All this has been demolished and replaced with industrial units but parts of Norfolk Place and Stafford Street remain and give us an idea of what it must have looked like. Very plain, narrow houses dominate Norfolk Street. Similar houses were to be found on the west side of the river on Fydell Street where a terrace was built in the 1830s for workers at the gas works (established in 1826). Over the next 20 years small groups spread further up Fydell Street and to the north up Castle Street.

Figure 38
The iron porch erected by William Howden at his property on Witham Bank East as a form of advertisement for his adjoining ironworks.
[DP165017]

Figure 39 (above)
The elegant doorway of Witham Bank House.
[DP165020]

Figure 40 (above, right)
The former Barge Inn, on the corner of Norfolk Street.
[DP151282]

Witham Bank West

The straightening of the Witham and the raised banks provided as flood defences gave new opportunities for the well-to-do wishing to move from the crowded centre of Boston to live in an area that was much more suburban in character. Here was a quiet location with broad river views, yet still within easy walking distance of the town centre. Villas began to be built from the 1820s along the west side of the river. Two large and handsome houses already occupied the east side, Witham Bank House and its neighbour. The new villas did not form a continuous row and there is still plenty of space between them. They were built over a period of some 30 years but all are essentially Regency in spirit. Set in generous gardens, in contrast to most houses of the period in Boston, they are all of two storeys although most are raised up on a basement storey to the level of the embanked path along the levee. Nos 16 and 48 are recognisably by the same hand, William Stainton (born c 1815), the most prolific builder/architect of Boston from the 1830s to the 1860s (Fig 41). No 16 was built in 1855 and No 48 in 1858, and are largely as built, No 48 retaining its original door (Fig 42). The only real difference between them was that No 16 was constructed with an oriel with fashionable plate-glass windows (although retaining cheaper small panes in its other windows). Other villas are in similar vein with console brackets to the doorcases, margin glazing, wave-moulded keystones and broad eaves. Some also have oriel bay windows and façades with some parts brought forward. Some similar villas were built on Haven Bank by the same builders. Taken as a whole, the villas represent a charming use of the riverside for residential purposes and many retain almost all their original architectural features.

On the south-west side of Boston, there was extensive development of workers' cottages in the 1820s. Whig landlords developed an area comprising Blue Street (13 houses built between 1826 and 1829 by Samuel Barnard, a Radical), King Street, Queen Street and Innocent Street, filled with small houses, many of which – other than Queen Street which has been widened as a principal route through the town – remain. Half of Liquorpond Street, developed after 1800 with narrow three-storey houses, linking the new streets to the High Street, also still exists. Almost all these houses, which were of the simplest design, have been extensively modernised in recent years.

As in many towns and cities, the rapidly expanding demand for working-class housing was met by building courts behind existing property, each containing a number of very small dwellings that were blind-backed (with just one window on each floor facing the court and none to the rear). Access to the courts was generally by a narrow passage. Such courts were built in the poorest parts of the town, in the Liquorpond/Blue Street and Rosegarth Street/Lincoln Lane areas. In 1866, four houses in Barwick's Court, Innocent Street, were closed as a nuisance. In layout, these were typical of court houses. There were two rooms in each house, one on each floor 8ft (2.4m) square, 6ft 4in (1.95m) high on the ground floor, and just 5–6ft (1.5–1.8m) high on the upper floor. The court was 6ft wide and there was only one shared privy for the four houses. These houses were occupied by the very poor: the census for 1861 reveals Stead's Passage behind Nos 17–18 Liquorpond Street to have been occupied by

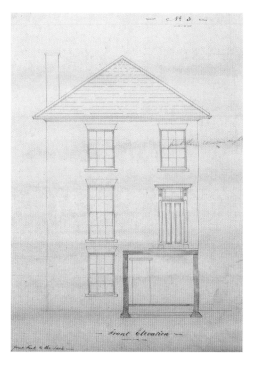

single women and children. Other occupants included fellmongers and charwomen while a pauper was recorded in Challen's Passage in 1841. These houses were the first to be demolished as slums and this type of building is nationally extremely rare. One pair of court dwellings survives in what was formerly Borland's Yard, behind Union Place (Fig 43). Although condemned in 1933, as part of Boston Corporation's slum clearance programme, they survived by being converted into a garage. Three more much altered examples in Heslam's Alley, facing the car park of the Baptist Chapel, were incorporated into the back of No 92 High Street (Fig 44). The houses in the rest of the alley were single storey with attics (which survived well into the 1960s) and the outline of one can clearly be seen in the front of the Sunday School of the Baptist Chapel, which it abutted.

Figure 41 (opposite, top)
A drawing by William Stainton depicting No 48 Witham Bank West.
[With the permission of Lincolnshire Archives]

Figure 42 (opposite, bottom)
No 48 Witham Bank West, built 1852, remains externally unchanged today as an elegant example of a riverside villa.
[DP151450]

Figure 43 (above)
Examples of former court houses, one room up and one room down, in what was Borland's Yard behind Union Place.
[DP161505]

Figure 44 (right)
Three former blind-back houses in Heslam's Alley, behind No 92 High Street.
[John Minnis]

Pen Street and development along Main Ridge

Development to the east of the medieval town followed in the early 19th century. It focussed on Pen Street where a series of three-storey semi-detached villas were linked by two-storey houses – in effect pavilions. The grandest pair in the road is Nos 23–5 which has the entrances set back so that it looks like a mansion and is placed so that it is the focus of the view from Grove Street opposite, developed at the same time. The houses in Pen Street have the fine proportions and detailing of doorcases seen in Witham Place, with both the pedimented Doric type and the Regency reeded style in evidence, together with the 'Boston' type (*see* p 37). Also notable is the use of very deep round-headed staircase windows. Although the grandest houses were built on the west side, there were numerous handsome smaller houses on the east side as well (Fig 45). The area has suffered from the intrusion of John Adams Way which led to the destruction of many houses to the east of Pen Street. Grove Street suffered too but an impressive group of three town houses survive on the north side (Fig 46). These have the margin lights so popular in Boston and 'Boston' type doorcases.

Figure 45
Nos 38–44A Pen Street. Typical of much late 18th and early 19th-century development in the area, these were tall narrow houses, mostly built by individual speculators, as may be seen by the breaks in the brickwork between each house. No 44A is a reconstruction.
[DP165423]

Figure 46
Nos 2–6 Grove Street, a terrace of three houses from
the early 19th century.
[DP161435]

Many of the houses in both streets have another characteristic feature, timber fascias below the eaves with dentilled mouldings.

A reminder that poverty was to be found side by side with affluence in almost all towns in the 19th century is to be found in Pen Street Yard, next to No 11 Pen Street. The yard was owned by the Lyell family, butcher's of Wide Bargate, between 1877 and 1922. The yard contained the butcher's slaughterhouse, together with, as listed in the 1877 conveyance, seven stables, carriage houses, a shoemaker's shop, piggeries, two poor cottages and, by 1882, the premises of Joseph Wing & Son who dealt in hides, skins and fat.[51] Wing himself lived at No 16 Pen Street, probably just far enough away to escape the inevitable odours of his trade. The two cottages in the yard contained two families, one of six and the other of four. The yard today is still recognisable, although the cottages are long gone. The slaughterhouse remains, still part of the premises of the butcher's at No 33, Wide Bargate. The area became notorious for prostitution and the *Boston & Louth Guardian* on 22 October 1856 reported that there had been a deputation from Bargate residents to the magistrates to complain of 'the abominable nuisances arising from that hot-bed of vice and profligacy, known as the Pen-Yard'.

The area to the east of Pen Street was decimated by John Adams Way and the break is clearly seen in Main Ridge, bisected by the new road. The eastern part of Main Ridge was lined with three-storey houses and shops, all pre-dating 1829. Again these were of plain appearance but have now been altered almost beyond recognition. However, one characteristic of most of these buildings still clearly to be seen is the way in which the roofs descend in a catslide at the rear, thus rendering what appears from the front to be a full three-storey building little more than a two-storey one with an additional top floor only one room deep. This is another distinctive local design detail seen elsewhere in Boston.

The first part of the area to be built by 1819, following the widening of Maud Foster Drain, was a group of two pairs and a single house on the east bank of the drain and with access along the waterside path, now known as Windsor Bank. These houses were large and had their doorways set back to the side, in the same way as some of the houses in Pen Street. Again they have had windows altered and bay windows inserted but enough remains to gain an impression of their appearance when built. Next to them is a terrace that followed soon after the sale of surplus land in 1820 following the widening of the drain (Fig 47).

No 41 reveals that these houses all originally had red-brick segmental arches to the ground-floor windows and most distinctive glazing bars which almost formed a fanlight within the window (replaced in 2014 with uPVC glazing that attempts to replicate the detail) (Fig 48). The same detail is to be seen at the Unitarian Chapel and was evidently another local characteristic of the period. The terrace was gradually extended along Windsor Bank and a further group of three-storey houses had these windows although none retain the original fenestration.

To the north of Spilsby Road, further scattered development took place along Horncastle Road and Willoughby Road on opposite banks of the drain with one of Boston's great landmarks, the Maud Foster Mill, being built in 1819. It is the only rival to St Botolph's in its impact on the town's skyline. A tower mill with an adjacent owner's house, it was built for the Reckitt family by Hull millwrights Norman & Smithson and continues to produce flour to this day, the last survivor of many mills in the area.

Figure 47 (above, left)
Houses on Windsor Bank dating from the 1820s and 1830s, overlooking the Maud Foster Drain.
[DP165005]

Figure 48 (above)
No 41 Windsor Bank. The elegant ground-floor window, the sole surviving example of its kind in this terrace of 1820s cottages, was replaced in uPVC in 2014.
[John Minnis]

The final area to see significant expansion in the early 19th century was that stretching along Spilsby Road to the north-east (Fig 49). In many towns, the best houses were located on the main routes in and out of them and Boston was no exception, but turnpike tollgates on Sleaford Road at the Carlton Road junction and on London Road at Black Sluice inhibited development in these directions for many years – that on Spilsby Road however was at Hilldyke, some two miles out of the town. Building stretched over many years with Spilsby Road not becoming fully built up until the 1930s. Among the first buildings to go up was Nos 76–82, a terrace of four houses with basements in fashionable white brick and a similar semi-detached pair to the west (Nos 72–4). Detailing calls to mind some of the houses on Witham Bank West with the use of two-panel doors, rectangular fanlights, and door surrounds with incised panels. Other villas soon followed, mostly variations on the theme of hipped roofs, white brick and classicism, often with margin light windows and leaning towards Italianate as the century progressed, acquiring heavier window surrounds, more elaborate

brackets and banding to the eaves. No 132 Elm House was built by William Stainton in the 1850s for his own occupation, still displaying a simple classicism in its design, although with showy large plate-glass windows (Fig 50). Many of the villas display both craftsmanship and originality of treatment: one half of the pair Nos 134–6, built in the early 1850s by Stainton, had a large and ornate conservatory installed in front of it towards the end of the century, while No 142 of 1861 had its ground floor set back to form a loggia and some extraordinary windows with large bosses at the junction of the mullions and transoms, a move towards high Victorian design.

Scattered development occurred to the south of the centre on and around Skirbeck Road. Thomas Dickinson, a woolstapler, developed an area immediately on the east bank of the Haven in phases between *c* 1827 and 1846. Much of the development, consisting of St John's Square, St John's Close, St John's Passage and along St John's Road was of cottages. However, one part of it, South Terrace, was intended for superior tenants and was a convex crescent of nine substantial houses in grey brick with handsome doorcases (Fig 51). Dickinson advertised them in the *Stamford Mercury* on 1 February 1832 as 'most delightfully situated on the River Witham, and commanding a most luxuriant view on the opposite bank, an extensive prospect of South-Place, High-street, Skirbeck Quarter, and the shipping in Boston Harbour, combining views superior to any in or about Boston … The whole will be found to be worth the attention of those who duly estimate their health, and know the value of a dry situation' although the claim that 'the whole of the premises are well drained into

the river' was somewhat at odds with the healthy aspect of South Terrace. The other elements of Dickinson's development have since been demolished.

Religious provision

Boston was unusual in that, until 1822, it possessed only the one great parish church of St Botolph's. A chapel of ease opened in 1822 in the High Street (demolished 1948) but it was not until 1861–4 that St James's Church (demolished 1970) was built in George Street at the centre of an area inhabited by railway workers. The suburb growing along Spilsby Road was in Skirbeck parish but some distance from St Nicholas's church and, in 1848, Holy Trinity was opened to serve that middle-class community (Fig 52). George Gilbert Scott, who had married his cousin Caroline Oldrid, a member of the important local Oldrid family, and already engaged on the restoration of St Botolph's, was commissioned. He designed a large church in Decorated Gothic, with an extensive set of good stained glass that has accrued since it was built.

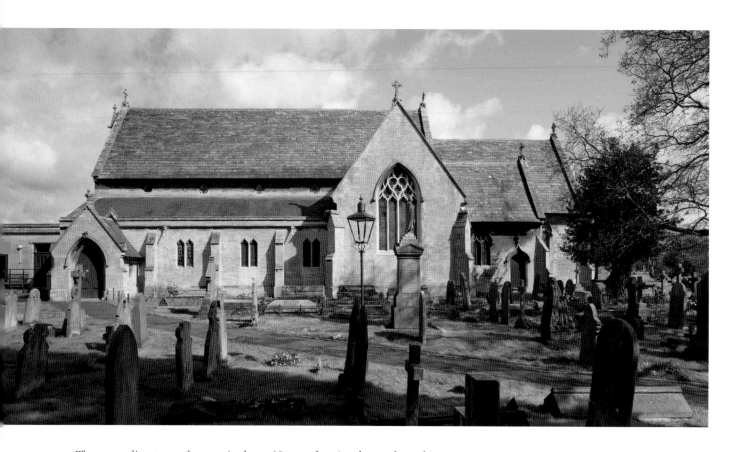

Figure 52
Holy Trinity, Spilsby Road (George Gilbert Scott, 1848).
[DP161501]

The expanding town also required new Nonconformist places of worship, partly because of increased population but also due to the frequent schisms that occurred among congregations.

A Methodist chapel was built in the northern part of Red Lion Street in 1808 and enlarged in 1818 to accommodate 1,100 worshippers. Despite its size, it proved inadequate and was superseded between 1839 and 1840. The old chapel was converted into a pair of semi-detached houses which were let to two Methodist ministers, one Wesleyan, the other Primitive, in which form it survives today, well disguised with uPVC windows, but standing out from its neighbours in the street by its much greater bulk. A pair of doorcases with large console brackets, presumably put in just after 1840 when the residential conversion was done, is a prominent feature of the white-brick façade. The 1839 Centenary Chapel, designed by John Marshall, who lived in nearby Witham Place, an architect member of the congregation, was built on a much larger site around the corner in the eastern part of Red Lion Street.

The Salem Particular Baptist Chapel, Liquorpond Street, was built in 1800 but has subsequently seen substantial alterations including re-fronting in 1902. It has been in commercial use for many years as has the Independent Chapel in Grove Street, which was built in 1819 by voluntary subscription. A schoolroom was added to the south in 1841 and both buildings were restored and renovated in 1876 by Mr Tait, an architect, when six more classrooms were added to the school. 1819 also saw the erection of a most handsome Unitarian chapel on Spain Lane, one of the best in the country (Fig 53). Its façade, although simple, was perfectly proportioned with round-headed windows with Gothic glazing bars that can also be found in other Boston buildings constructed at the same time, notably the Barge Inn and houses along Maud Foster Drain.

The other surviving churches of this period include the Roman Catholic St Mary's Church, Horncastle Road, a plain, rather box-like structure of 1827, the appearance of which has not been helped by an addition of 1974. It retains its attractive presbytery with a reeded doorcase. The large brick-built Gothic General Baptist Chapel, High Street, 1837, was enlarged with side galleries in 1841 and gains greatly in appearance from its being set back from the road behind a railed courtyard (Fig 54).

Figure 53
The Unitarian Chapel, Spain Lane, 1819, with the Gothic glazing to its façade. The view is looking across John Adams Way, showing its impact on this, one of the finest buildings in Boston.
[DP165395]

Figure 54
The General Baptist Chapel, High Street, 1837. The galleries to each side were added in 1841.
[DP160407]

Public institutions

Most of Boston's surviving public buildings date from the second half of the 19th century but some earlier ones remain, among them, the original building of the Bluecoat charity school, much rebuilt, stands in Chapel Street and still bears a large oval plaque on the first floor, giving the date of construction as 1804. It was in use until 1876.

Only a fragment of the Union Workhouse of 1837 remains, a single-storey Italianate front range that is now on the fringes of the dock area and is almost surreally dwarfed by the row of grain bins standing immediately behind it. The building was designed by G G Scott at the start of his career when he was in partnership as Scott & Moffat, in which capacity he designed a great many similar structures.

Figure 55
The Sessions House (Charles Kirk, 1841–3).
[DP165394]

The other principal public building of the period is the Sessions House, its Tudor Gothic style, golden stone and castellated parapets well suited to its location beside St Botolph's (Fig 55). Built from 1841 to 1843 and designed by Charles Kirk of Sleaford, it is very similar in appearance to the Sessions House he built for Spalding, which was opened in 1842. Disused as a courthouse since the 1990s, it retains a remarkably intact interior. Construction was in part fireproof as seen in the jack-arches visible on the ground floor and in iron doors. The judge's parlour and retiring rooms have good light fittings, panelling and fireplaces, all in the Gothic style, and the courtroom has a splendid roof with timber trusses with openwork Gothic motifs supported on carved bosses depicting angels, lions and other creatures.

Also Gothic was the cemetery in Horncastle Road, opened in 1854. It was designed by the Darlington architect J P Pritchett, best known for his magnificent classical Huddersfield railway station, but who also undertook many cemeteries. A lodge, chapels and some fine monuments combine to form a distinctively Victorian environment.

The Great Northern Railway (GNR) came to Boston in 1848 and the town became, for a period, one of the key points on the system and the railway, its largest employer of labour. There was an intention for Boston to become the principal locomotive and rolling stock works for the GNR and it could potentially have occupied the place that Doncaster was to hold. Although this did not in the event happen, Boston was for many years a major junction with the headquarters of the District Engineers and the GNR occupying large tracts of land on the west side of the town with sidings, the engineers' yard, locomotive shed and goods yards. The original station was of timber and part of the building survived at least into the 1960s. A permanent station building was built in 1850, a straightforward single-storey structure in white brick with a portico, Italianate in style, like all the early GNR stations designed by Henry Goddard of Lincoln.

The land between the station and the town was soon occupied by streets of small houses for railway workers. Station Street was laid wide to form a grand approach to the station but, as its other end began in the slums of Lincoln Lane, that ambition was frustrated. In Skirbeck Quarter, the first houses to be built south of the turnpike toll bar were provided for workers who could easily walk to work in the various railway premises that extended northwards from the South Forty-Foot Drain.

4

Boston 1860–1914

From the 1860s, the lingering Georgian influence seen in much of Boston's domestic architecture was finally banished to be replaced by a tough looking series of buildings in harsh red brick whose distinguishing feature was the use of heavy brick corbelling below the eaves. The style was particularly associated with Samuel Sherwin (1835–1900), a builder who had a great impact on the town, not only putting up buildings to the designs of others but also designing many himself. Following work in Liverpool with Lewis Hornblower and Édouard André at the time they were laying out Sefton Park (opened in 1872), he joined William Stainton's building firm. He continued the business from 1873 until his death in 1900, when his son took over, running it until 1925. Sherwin, whose premises were at No 63–67 Wide Bargate (Fig 56), was a major figure in 19th-century Boston: a JP, Charity trustee, Chairman of the Gas, Light and Coke company, and owner of Shodfriars Hall. He employed 69 men and six boys directly in 1871 and, in addition to his extensive operations in Boston, also carried out much building work in other parts of the country.

The other major contributor to the appearance of Boston in the second half of the century was William Henry Wheeler (1832–1915). Wheeler was an engineer, architect and antiquarian best known for *A History of the Fens of South Lincolnshire*. He was appointed borough and harbour engineer to the Corporation in 1861 and was subsequently responsible for public buildings and those of the new port. He may also have carried out residential and commercial work in the town on his own account (he is known to be responsible for the staircase at No 116 High Street). Other builders were William Greenfield of Union Place and John T Barber of No 114 High Street who was said in 1910 to have erected large numbers of villas, terraced houses, shops and cottages, including houses in the High Street and Argyle Street. We are fortunate that a substantial collection of drawings from Sherwin & Sons (including many from William Stainton) are held in Lincolnshire Archives but, in the absence of surviving Building Regulations plans, it is impossible to identify very much work by other local architects and builders.

Houses

The earliest example of the Sherwin style appears to be Leighton House of 1875 (significantly just two years after Sherwin had assumed full control of his building

The Ordnance Survey 1:10,560 map, published in 1906, shows that, despite Boston's commercial importance in the 19th century, the town had not expanded its built-up area greatly. Much of the town was still only a short walk from open country.

business following the departure of Stainton) on Sleaford Road which has neo-Jacobean shaped gables, much terracotta decoration and tall chimneys with tall fin-like projections in brick emphasising their height. The theme is picked up by No 5 Haven Bank of 1877 (Fig 57). This is marked on the elevation drawings as being the work of William Thomas, architect, (about whom nothing is known, other than that he also designed the former Anderson's feather works in Trinity Street, also built by Sherwin, *see* Fig 73), but the style is that adopted by Sherwin as his own. It shows dramatically the differing styles of Stainton and Sherwin – while the villa is in general form and layout similar to its earlier neighbours on Witham Bank and Haven Bank by Stainton (*see* pp 39–40), who had retained his allegiance to the Regency style of his youth to the end, Thomas employed a much coarser treatment of detail more in tune with prevailing taste. It had heavy eaves corbels, an ornate bay window and a fretwork porch. The windows too were very different from the small-paned sashes seen in the 1850s, having plate-glass casements of highly distinctive design (Fig 58). A series of semi-detached and terraced houses on the south side of Sleaford Road, Nos 14–16, built by Sherwin in 1879, and Norman Villas of 1880 are all in the same vein. These and Nos 22–4 have façades built in the fashionable white brick with eaves and bands of red brick and terracotta while the terrace of nine houses 'The Park' of 1887 bears a large terracotta panel celebrating Queen Victoria's Golden Jubilee in the gable of the end house.

Sherwin was, however, outclassed by Wheeler who in 1887 designed a house for himself in London Road (Fig 59), on the edge of the built-up area. From the exterior, the house appeared quite heavy with the usual red brick and terracotta seen elsewhere in Boston. Inside, the decoration was at the forefront of contemporary thinking in interior design. It is a riot of ornate timberwork, tiling (Fig 60), much of it specially designed, and stained glass. Fireplaces have extraordinary beasts that look as if they come from the pages of a fantasy novel (Fig 61). Although the house was in institutional use for many years and is currently St George's Preparatory School, it retains the bulk of this decoration and is the finest Victorian interior in the town.

From the 1880s, there was further extensive development of three-bedroom terraced and semi-detached housing, mainly on the west and north sides of Boston (Figs 62 and 63). These houses generally had small front gardens and bay windows, usually entirely of wood and, in many cases, of relatively elaborate

Figure 56 (above)
No 63 Wide Bargate, once part of Samuel Sherwin's premises with the former site of his builder's yard behind and to the side of it. The grand classical temple façade hides what is essentially a small cottage.
[DP161453]

Figure 57 (opposite, top)
No 5 Haven Bank, from the contract drawing by William Thomas.
[With the permission of Lincolnshire Archives]

Figure 58 (opposite, bottom)
No 5 Haven Bank, 1877, showing the ornate joinery and brickwork.
[DP151294]

carpentry. This decorative work evolved into a distinctive local type by the late 1890s and it is most in evidence in the semi-detached villas built around the new Central Park from 1894 to 1907. The upper sashes of the bay windows of these have pointed tops to the glazed lights while the doors have a profusion of coloured glass. These features are also to be seen on some houses in Sleaford Road: Nos 58 Ophirton House and No 60 Pittsburg House (Fig 64).

Other characteristics are houses that appear to be a single dwelling of three bays with a central doorway but are paired with a second doorway on one of the side elevations, masking the fact that they are actually semi-detached. Extremely ornate joinery is also to be found on many of the houses surrounding the park. Examples include curved shaped brackets supporting gabled dormers, copiously adorned with finials, on Kingswood and Eastwood of 1907, Norfolk Street (Fig 65). Similar gables combine with trefoil headed windows on Thirlmere and Alderside on Tawney Street to produce an even more fanciful effect. A number of these houses are larger with significant back extensions and their superior nature is indicated in the use of terracotta decoration such as the Greek key bands on Oakleigh and Hillsborough of 1905. Some houses such as Aberdour and Montrose have carved leaves set amongst the mouldings of the entablature to the bay windows and stylised thorns incised below while other motifs typical of the period appear on tiling to dado height in some doorways in the area.

More substantial houses went up along the north side of Sleaford Road, as infill development on Spilsby Road (although much of the south side remained undeveloped until the 1920s) and along Wyberton West Road. Sleaford Road has a spectacular collection of villas on its north side. Among them are Nos 55–61, two pairs of large semi-detached houses with half-timbering in the gables built in the early 1880s, No 63 Normanhurst with especially ornate windows, complete with leaded lights in the upper parts, No 65 Teviot Lodge (Fig 66), one of the most striking with a tall hall window and massive chimneys rising from the walls and finally No 67 Lynton House, with shaped gables.

Samuel Sherwin, as well as designing and building houses for individuals and developers, also engaged in estate development himself. He acquired a wedge of land bordering what is now Queen's Road, facing the Maud Foster Drain, and had Lockwood & Mawson, the noted Bradford-based architectural practice – responsible for Saltaire, amongst much other work – make a series of villa designs in 1879 (Fig 67). All had the same basic form in red brick with a

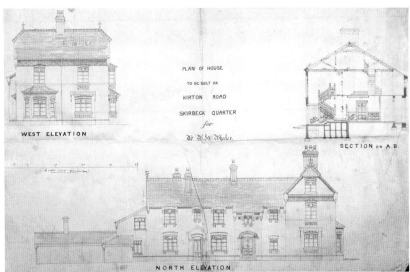

Figure 59 (left)
W H Wheeler's house, No 126 London Road, 1887,
contract drawing.
[With the permission of Lincolnshire Archives]

Figure 60 (below, left)
No 126 London Road, decorative tile.
[DP151352]

Figure 61 (below)
No 126 London Road, details of the extraordinary
decoration of the fire surround.
[DP151367]

Figure 62 (above)
Many of Boston's smaller terraces of cottages bear plaques giving their name and date of construction. The most unusual must be Sea on Land Terrace in Main Ridge East which owes its name to the developer, George Aspland, a well-known fairground proprietor whose premises were adjacent. He named it after the latest ride produced by Savages of King's Lynn.
[DP161456]

Figure 63 (above, right)
A rare example of formal planning in Boston: Tower Street, a new residential road constructed in the 1870s on the west side of the Haven, was aligned directly with the tower of St Botolph's.
[DP165489]

Figure 64 (right)
No 58 Ophirton House and No 60 Pittsburgh House, Sleaford Road.
[DP161477]

gable facing the road but varied in their decorative treatment. In the event, four villas were constructed the following year, one, No 9 Thirlmere House, for Sherwin's own occupation. Each differed slightly from its neighbour: the most elaborate was No 8 Dyke House with a splendid timber porch with a half-hipped roof. Sherwin's house was plainer but with a garden that extended around the back of the other houses in the road (Fig 68). None of them exactly matched the Lockwood & Mawson drawings and it would seem that Sherwin mixed and matched elements from them and slightly simplified the designs. They survive in largely original condition and show how well variety could be achieved in juggling components of what was essentially the same design.

The late 19th-century houses of Boston, while they may not be in the forefront of the development of architectural style, nevertheless have a strong character which is particularly noticeable in the detailing of timber porches, bays, doors and windows and in the employment of decorative brickwork (Fig 69). They, alongside their simpler Georgian and Regency predecessors, contribute greatly to the appearance of the town and are a significant asset that deserves to be better appreciated.

Figure 65 (above, left)
Kingswood and Eastwood, Norfolk Street.
[John Minnis]|

Figure 66 (above)
No 65 Teviot Lodge, Sleaford Road.
[DP161479]

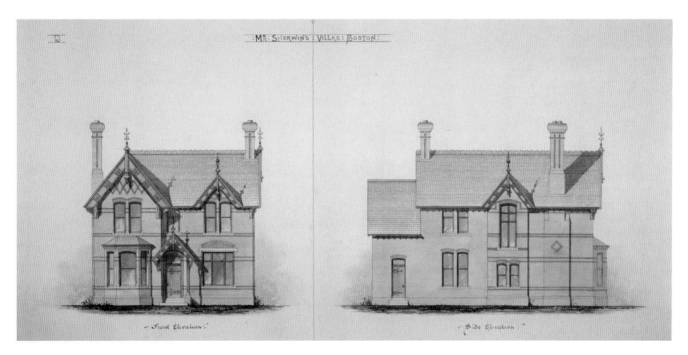

: Mr : Sherwin's : Villas : Boston :

- Front Elevation -   - Side Elevation -

Figure 67 (above)
A villa design by Lockwood & Mawson for Samuel Sherwin, 1879.
[With the permission of Lincolnshire Archives]

Figure 68 (right)
No 8 Dyke House, Queens Road, the Lockwood & Mawson design as adapted by Samuel Sherwin. Since this photograph was taken the garage has been demolished and the garden to the left built over.
[John Minnis]

Figure 69
Some houses retained elements of classical design until well into the second half of the 19th century as here on Willoughby Road. The classical door surround recalls those on houses of the 1850s, as does the moulded lintel, while margin lights became popular and were retro-fitted to many houses in Boston. Such details, when they are as well maintained as these, greatly enhance the town's appearance.
[DP165487]

Religion

Local Anglicans long thought that the Skirbeck Quarter was not well served by the distant St Nicholas's, resulting in the construction of a corrugated-iron church, St Thomas's, on London Road in 1885. The intention was always to replace it with a permanent structure and in 1912 one of the finest church architects of the period, Temple Moore, produced designs in a simple Arts and Crafts inspired style. Everything about the building is at first sight simple and the effect is one of considerable subtlety (Fig 70). The walls are rendered externally and the building is somewhat domestic in appearance when seen from the south with the long tiled slopes of the roof and the unadorned mullioned windows of the porch and the transept (Fig 71). A late addition to St Botolph's was the Blenkin Memorial Hall of 1893, a pleasant exercise in a broadly Arts and Crafts style by W Samuel Weatherley of London (who also designed the war memorial in Wide Bargate in 1921), built behind the 17th-century Church House in Wormgate.

Figure 70 (right)
*St Thomas's Church, London Road
(Temple Moore, 1912).*
[DP151393]

Figure 71 (below)
*The door to the vestry of St Thomas's showing
the almost domestic character of some parts
of the building.*
[DP151390]

The Nonconformists too undertook a building programme. Among the survivors is the former Primitive Methodist chapel, West Street. This was built from 1865 to 1856 to a design by Bellamy & Hardy of Lincoln. It suffered a disastrous fire and was rebuilt by T & C H Howdill of Leeds in 1898. Thomas Howdill was a prolific chapel architect whose practice, carried out in partnership with his son and centred on Leeds and the West Riding, extended over much of the country. The building is very much in the classical idiom favoured in the mid-19th century and it probably reproduced many of the features of its predecessor. It closed in 1965 and is now a supermarket.

The 1839 Centenary Wesleyan Chapel (*see* p 48) was burnt down in 1909 and parts of the remaining walls may have been incorporated into the new chapel by Gordon & Gunton, opened in the following year and one of the finest of its period in England (Fig 72). This has a dramatic convex façade with two massive towers at each end of it. These are topped with cupolas with paired columns that push out of the angles to heighten the baroque feel of the building. The classicism of the chapel contrasts with the red-brick Gothic of the Sunday Schools behind it which survived the fire and were designed by Hull-based architects Gelder & Kitchen in 1898. The interiors of both the chapel and Sunday Schools are spectacular with galleries cantilevered out into the body of the chapel and a fine timber roof in the Sunday Schools.

Industry and commerce

Boston's industry revolved around the products of the surrounding agricultural areas which were funnelled through the town and its related extensive market and port functions.

Perhaps the most significant event in the development of Boston's economy in the 19th century was the relocation of the port from the site it had occupied since medieval times, along the Haven in the centre of the town, to an entirely new location to the south of the town where there was room for enclosed docks of a modern type, capable of dealing with large ships, and with suitable warehousing and rail access. Boston's maritime traffic had been in decline for years and the arrival of the railway in 1848 had finished off much of the coastal trade. The docks were built and owned by the Corporation and were part of a scheme that included a new cut two miles in length to the Wash. They opened in 1884 and the architectural work was carried out by the Corporation's architect W H Wheeler. The new docks were a success and led to a revival in the town's maritime trade and, until the 1920s, a great expansion in deep-sea fishing which became one of Boston's major industries.

The many ships based in Boston during the 19th century ensured that there was a great demand for rope and three rope-walks, which were long narrow sites on which the rope was made, are shown on the 1886–7 1.500 Town Plan. One, located at the end of Spain Lane running due east to west along the boundary of land owned by the Fydell family, was in use by 1829 when it was run by a Mr Thorley. The south stand of Boston United Football Club is almost exactly on much of its site today. A second, also in existence by 1829, ran along the boundary today located between the Boston Shopping Park and the back

Figure 72
*Centenary Wesleyan Chapel, Red Lion Street
(Gordon & Gunton, 1910).*
[DP161474]

gardens on the south side of Hartley Street. Perhaps the most intriguing of all is that along the south side of Hospital Lane. Here the rope-walk ran along the top edge of a field adjoining the backs of a row of small semi-detached cottages spaced at intervals along the road with large gaps between them occupied by their gardens and privies. Each cottage had a single-storey addition that backed directly on to the rope-walk. The cottages, now much altered, are still there but the rope-walk itself has been taken into the field.

Besides the grain warehouses lining the Haven, little remains of Boston's once flourishing industries. The most spectacular survival is the former Anderson's feather works in Trinity Street, designed by William Thomas and built by Sherwin & Sons in 1879 with a grand three-storey façade of considerable elaboration with a giant swan high above the cornice as its crowning glory (Fig 73). The office buildings of Tuxford's ironworks, once one of the major manufacturers of agricultural machinery in East Anglia, at the junction of Fishtoft Road and Windsor Bank, are small beer by comparison but are a reminder of what was once a major contributor to the town's economy. More substantial survivals are the manager's house, boardroom and clerk's office of the Boston Gas, Light and Coke Company (Fig 74). Boston had produced gas from 1826 but the present buildings date from between 1868 and 1871 and are robustly Victorian in red brick with polychromatic banding of a vivid kind, the offices having a grand porch. All this was the work of the ubiquitous Samuel Sherwin, himself the Chairman of the company at the time.

Many shops too were remodelled in the latest styles from the 1860s onwards. The much more flamboyant designs of this period stand out, as they were intended to do, amongst their rather more demure Georgian and Regency neighbours in the High Street, West Street, Wide Bargate and the Market Place. In West Street, Nos 27–9, Cheers' outfitters premises from 1930 until 1985 – and still bearing their name painted high up on the side of the building – has a tall exuberant terracotta façade with a Dutch gable and striking blocked surrounds to the upper floor windows (Fig 75). Nos 51–3 a little further west has an almost oriental feel to it, with a tall oriel window on the splayed corner that terminates in a conical cap. In the High Street, an oriel window is again a prominent feature of a pair of shops designed by Samuel Sherwin in 1883 at Nos 8 (Fig 76) and 10–12, the latter for the gunsmiths Slingsby's, who occupied premises on the site from the 1860s until 1965. Also probably the work of Sherwin is the shop on the

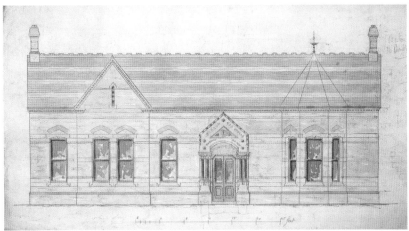

Figure 73 (left)
The former Anderson's feather works, Trinity Street
(William Thomas, 1879).
[DP161504]

Figure 74 (below, left)
The offices of the Boston Gas, Light and Coke Company
(Samuel Sherwin, 1868–71).
[With the permission of Lincolnshire Archives]

Figure 75 (below)
Detail of the terracotta façade of Nos 27–9 West Street,
for many years the premises of Messrs Cheers,
outfitters.
[John Minnis]

corner of Wide Bargate and Pen Street, No 43, with its stepped gable and tall chimneys whose stacks burst out of the flank wall of the building. Plans survive of its neighbour at No 41, confirming that it was designed by Sherwin in 1876 after a lengthy process in which he submitted various proposals to the client, a Mr Robinson.

Commerce too was served by some impressive new buildings. The bankers moved from their traditional location at the south end of High Street to premises in the centre of town with a number in the Market Place (*see* p 83) and Gee, Wise & Co just over the other side of the Haven (Fig 77) adjacent to the refurbished White Hart Hotel (Fig 78).

Public buildings

Many of Boston's public buildings date from the second half of the century. The most interesting were the product of private enterprise rather than expenditure by the Corporation. Shodfriars Hall (*see* Fig 105) is perhaps the most spectacular example. The delightful Freemasons' Hall in Main Ridge West was given a façade of superb quality in the Egyptian style between 1860 and 1861, many years after the craze for Egyptian was at its height in the 1820s and 1830s (Fig 79). The style was, however, always closely associated with freemasonry which would explain its use here. The portico was derived from the Temple of Dandour in Nubia, while the two columns were based on those at Edfou and Philae. The Corporation provided a public park (later the People's Park), laid out by W H Wheeler along the banks of the Haven, which was opened in 1871. It took in what had been the Bath Gardens dating from the 1830s and was closed when the timber quays at the port expanded to take over the land in the 1930s. Adjacent to the park was the Boston Cottage Hospital of 1875 by Wheeler, replacing a pair of converted cottages in Stanbow Lane. This lasted until the 1970s when the Pilgrim Hospital opened. The Corporation Baths at the north end of the People's Park, with men's and women's baths, six hot saltwater baths and a family bath, opened in 1880. The baths was also by Wheeler in his characteristically heavy style. Today, only the frontage building remains. Most of the board schools have gone but two historic schools still stand, the combined Laughton's and Bluecoat School (1876) and St James Middle Class Girls' School (1896).

Figure 76
No 8 High Street (Samuel Sherwin, 1883), an example of his commercial work.
[With the permission of Lincolnshire Archives]

Figure 77
*A grand palazzo front was employed for the Gee,
Wise & Co Bank in High Street, built in 1863–4.
The architect is unknown although the plans
survive in Lincolnshire Archives.*
[DP161444]

Figure 78
*The White Hart became the premier hotel in the town
and was extended to take over the building seen on
the right, which was recased c 1878 in an elaborate
confection of moulded stucco, disguising the plain
Georgian structure underneath.*
[DP161446]

Figure 79
The Freemasons' Hall, Main Ridge West, 1860–1.
[DP161402]

By far the largest public building to be erected in Boston was the new Municipal Buildings in West Street, built in 1902 (Fig 80). The Corporation turned to a local architect, James Rowell, to design it, rather than employing a major national figure. Rowell, of Carlton Road, Boston, had trained under W H Wheeler and his known work is limited to the science laboratory at the Boston Grammar School, Boston's board schools and the infirmary and other buildings at the Boston Workhouse (demolished). The result was a building impressive in scale but less assured in its detailing: broadly Jacobean with plenty of scroll mouldings and a little dated with its French Second Empire mansard roof

Figure 80
The Municipal Buildings, West Street
(James Rowell, 1902).
[DP165002]

behind the central gable which would have been fashionable 30 years earlier. But it certainly had the necessary grandeur for its purpose and the council chamber and the former police court, both with oak panelling and other woodwork carried out in Sherwin & Son's Boston yard, are splendid. Although the council chamber is not large, the massive chimneypiece (which incorporates Boston's coat of arms as do the stained-glass windows), the coved ceiling with elaborate fibrous plasterwork in the style of the 16th century and an arcade of round-headed arches inject the right degree of municipal pomp. The building provided, besides council offices, a police station and police court, a fire station, a public library and premises for the school of art.

The town's first purpose-built Post Office, designed and built by Sherwin, opened in the High Street in 1885. It had a short life, although it still exists as a Wetherspoons pub, and was replaced in 1907 by a most handsome Edwardian baroque structure in Wide Bargate with a domed turret on the corner and plenty of Portland stone dressings contrasting with the brick used elsewhere on its exterior (Fig 81). Extended in the 1930s, it was closed in 2013 and awaits a new use. Along with Tunnard House, Cammack's and the Red Cow (*see* Figs 90 and 91), it is one of the varied group of buildings that help to give Wide Bargate so much character as townscape.

Figure 81
The Post Office, Wide Bargate (1907).
[DP165418]

5

Boston from 1920

There was relatively little building in the centre of Boston between the wars but one local architect produced some distinctive work. Hedley Adams Mobbs (1891–1969) was a man of a great many parts. Besides his career as an architect, he was a *Punch* cartoonist, a crack rifleman at Bisley, played football for Cambridge City and was also known as a ragtime pianist, beekeeper, horticulturalist and artist. In his later years, he also invented a headlamp that automatically dipped itself, and devoted much of his time working on what he termed the 'bee-house' – a design for a house made up of hexagonal units that was inspired by the honeycombs made by bees. He is best remembered for his magnificent stamp collection that owed much to his friendship with Sir Ewerby Thorpe, King George V's Keeper of the King's Philately.[52]

Mobbs' most striking building, still in its original ownership, is Cammack's furniture store, Wide Bargate (Fig 82), on a site that has been occupied by a succession of three furniture makers and dealers since 1840. Cammack & Sons Ltd was founded in 1919 and the new building went up from 1931 to 1932. It stood out immediately because of its height: it was steel framed and incorporated what was claimed to be the first lift in Boston. Its three bay windows, extending over three floors, gave Cammack's a powerful vertical emphasis and the plain panel above, in which the name Cammack was enclosed in a frame with sunburst motifs at each end, completed an effective composition. Buildings of this period are often neglected and unsympathetically altered but the lines of Cammack's have been enhanced by an appropriate and tasteful colour scheme. The new shop was so much more modern than anything else in Boston that the draper's Keightley's rebuilt their premises in the High Street in imitation of Cammack's.

Mobbs also rebuilt Mason's shoe shop (now Clarks) in Strait Bargate in a moderne style, this time with more of a horizontal emphasis to suit the broad plot (Fig 83) His other work included the rather natty gates (1932) to Central Park with their waves and sunbursts and the adjacent wall and pavilions which use tiles on end (creasing) as decoration in an Arts and Crafts manner (Fig 84). Central Park was acquired by Boston Corporation in 1919 for public use: it had been a private park where cricket had been played since the 1840s. It supplemented the People's Park as the only public open space in the centre of the town. The Zion Methodist church in Brothertoft Road (1934) is an example of restrained modernism in red brick and has a bowed façade with tall windows.

The route of John Adams Way, seen from the east, as it cuts through Boston, close to the historic centre. [28410/091]

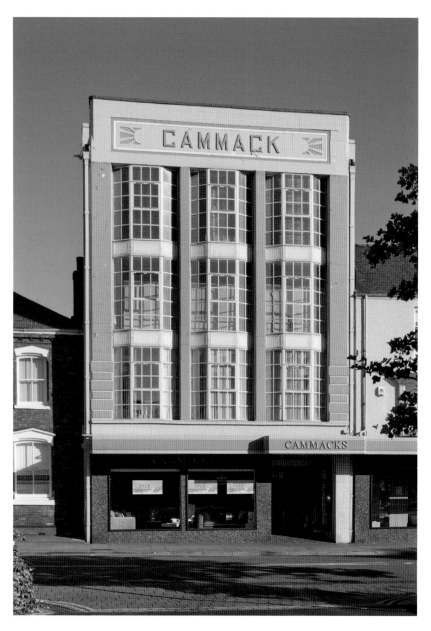

Figure 82 (opposite, left)
Cammack's, Wide Bargate (Hedley Mobbs, 1931–2).
[DP160486]

Figure 83 (opposite, top right)
The former Mason's shoe shop (now Clarks)
(Hedley Mobbs, 1933).
[DP165485]

Figure 84 (opposite, bottom right)
The screen wall and gates to Central Park
(Hedley Mobbs, 1932).
[John Minnis]

Figure 85 (above)
Boston Library, built as Holland County Council Offices
(W E Norman Webster, 1925–7).
[John Minnis]

Other than Mobbs' work, there was little new architecture in the town. Marks & Spencer had a stripped classical building put up in the 1930s on a prominent site in the Market Place. It retains its now rare pre-war shopfront. Other striking additions to the town were the two cinemas, the Odeon in South Square and the Regal, West Street, both now demolished. The County Offices for Holland County Council, built to a very traditional neo-Tudor design by W E Norman Webster of Spalding in 1925 to 1927, had an ashlar façade, intended to harmonise with the nearby Sessions House. On the abolition of the Council in 1974 with local government reorganisation, the building became Boston's public library (Fig 85).

The growth of popular motoring led to the establishment of several garages in the town. The largest was Holland Brothers on Wide Bargate on a site that had formerly been occupied by a succession of wheelwrights and carriage makers from 1826 onwards. A vast shed-like building went up in the 1920s that was typical of many garages of the period in that it had a broad unobstructed interior with plenty of space for car parking, as well as repairs and car sales. At that time, cars tended to be parked under cover rather than on the street and parking was provided by private enterprise rather than the local authority. The building still exists as an Iceland supermarket. Another garage of the same period, similar in layout but smaller, also remains around the corner in Tawney Street. More spectacular was the garage, now a tyre, brake and exhaust depot, on London Road in the Skirbeck Quarter, near the roundabout with the A16, which has a curved brick tower, very much of its time.

Perhaps the greatest change to Boston between the wars was that the formerly compact town in which one could walk into fields just east of South Street was encircled by a mass of suburban growth. This was particularly evident on the east side where the houses extended to the parish boundary. The suburban developments were much like those elsewhere with small, mainly semi-detached, houses set in areas that grew up with little attempt at planning. The first council estate was built on the west side at Westfield Avenue in 1926 and a large one grew up in the late 1930s on the west side of the River Witham as an extension of Carlton Road. Higher-quality houses were constructed along Spilsby Road to fill up the undeveloped frontages. These were well-detailed substantial houses of very traditional appearance that in some cases looked more like their Edwardian neighbours than houses of the 1920s and 1930s.

Since 1945

The post-war period initially saw little change in the built environment of
Boston. Agriculture continued to be the major source of employment in the area
and local industry continued to thrive with new industries springing up. Shops
and much industry remained locally owned.

Few new buildings were constructed – the most notable in the centre
being the new premises for the Nottingham Co-operative Society in West Street
(Fig 86). These were built in two stages: the first part, a food hall, designed 'on
American super market lines' opened in 1957 [53] and the second, on the other
side of Paddock Grove, had a public hall, restaurant, chemist's, shoe shop and
hairdresser's and opened two years later. The buildings were strikingly different
to anything previously built in Boston and had something of the feel of the
Festival of Britain to them. The department store for Messrs H E Keightley Ltd,
Drapers & Furnishers, almost opposite the Co-op, replaced the former White
Horse Commercial Hotel at the corner of Emery Lane and West Street, between
1958 and 1959. Significantly, the architect was a local man, Alan Meldrum, his

Figure 86
Co-operative store, West Street (1959).
[DP161507]

first large job on his own account. 1959 also saw the new Waterfield department store built in Bargate, again the work of a local architectural practice, L D Tomlinson & Partners.

The process of slum clearance in the area begun in 1933 regained momentum and was largely completed by the early 1970s. An ambitious plan had been drawn up in 1968 by Arthur Ling & Associates (Ling had been Chief Architect at Coventry and was responsible for much of that city's post-war reconstruction). On the site of the tightly packed Rosegarth Street and Lincoln Lane, arose a series of buildings all designed by Ling in red brick and slate: the police headquarters (since reclad), a DHSS building, a supermarket and a bus station and car park, all built between 1974 and 1976. The development was described by Nicholas Antram in the Lincolnshire volume of the *Buildings of England* series as lacking a 'visual focus', the landscaping 'depressingly without a sense of place' and, as a whole, 'a wasted opportunity'.[54] As the one area of comprehensive redevelopment in the town, this harsh judgment must stand but at least the area does not impinge much on West Street which retains considerable character.

Even more damaging were some demolitions in the Market Place. The destruction of the Peacock and Royal Hotel (Fig 87) in 1966, to be replaced by some particularly bland shops can only be described as tragic. No 60 Market Place (timber framed with a Georgian façade) was among those buildings selected for illustration in the *Architects' Journal* by SAVE Britain's Heritage in 1975 as examples of notable buildings demolished in European Architectural Heritage Year. Further shops were lost in Strait Bargate between 1969 and 1971 as part of Oldrid's redevelopment and the Red Lion Hotel was demolished in 1963.

Elsewhere in the town, redundant warehouses along the River Witham were demolished on South Street and South Square. The London warehouse, built by the Corporation in 1817 (demolished 1951), similar in much of its detailing to the still extant Public warehouse on the west bank of the river, was the most significant casualty but the Packhouse Quay (demolished 1963) and Johnson's warehouses, together with the last part of Ingelow House, were also notable losses. The High Street and London Road lost many early and important buildings. Nos 41–3 High Street, a 16th-century house with a distinctive crow-stepped gable was a major loss of 1972, not just architecturally, but in terms of townscape as its demolition left an ugly break in the street that is still used

merely for surface car parking. Further south, numerous Georgian houses disappeared on both the High Street and London Road.

Until the 1960s, Boston was served by express trains to London that ran directly south towards Peterborough. A reduction in rail services has led to the disappearance of much of the railway infrastructure since the 1970s. However, the principal station building (although it has lost the covered train sheds behind) and the West Street Junction signal box (1874) survive, together with a goods shed of 1903, a sacking store and a few buildings from the 1894 engineers' yard, converted to other purposes.

The biggest change was the continued expansion of the town's residential suburbs from the 1950s onwards and these now extend southwards to Wyberton, almost halfway to Hubbert's Bridge to the west and far beyond Skirbeck to the east. A large council estate was built north of Skirbeck centred around Woad Farm Road in the 1950s. The expansion in population led to the need for new public facilities to serve it, including new schools and, perhaps the most prominent addition to the town's skyline, the Pilgrim Hospital on its northern edge, with its 10-storey ward block. The hospital, in an uncompromisingly modern style, was built between 1967 and 1974 but there have been substantial additions since. It was sited so as not to impact on the town's skyline but the multi-storey Post Office telephone exchange added in the 1970s was an out of scale intrusion, which, although it was tucked away on the back land behind Strait Bargate, nevertheless was all too visible from much of the town and has exercised a malign influence ever since.

Moving to the southern part of Boston, the war years saw the construction of a massive steel-framed and concrete-clad grain silo (Fig 88) that remains a landmark and the Black Sluice pumping station, an imposing structure in red brick controlling the waters of the South Forty-Foot Drain, was built in 1949 and extended in 1966 (Fig 89). Although entirely functional, both structures are impressive and dominate the southern end of London Road. The port area saw significant change after the 1960s. Formerly with open access to the public, in 1990, like many other British ports, it became a closed area. The warehouses designed by Wheeler in the 1880s were demolished to be replaced by modern sheds and open quaysides. The port expanded to take in the former public park and traffic switched largely to road, the HGVs adding to the congestion on Skirbeck Road. Today the port's business continues to grow. The rail link via the

Figure 87
The Peacock & Royal Hotel, Market Place (demolished),
photographed in September 1962.
[AA62/07554]

Figure 88
The wartime grain silo and the docks area.
[John Minnis]

Figure 89
Black Sluice pumping station (1949, extended 1966).
[John Minnis]

swing bridge over the Haven is still in use for a daily freight train and the octagonal control cabin remains a distinctive feature of London Road.

The changes that had the greatest impact on Boston however, were the construction of the Haven Bridge in 1965 and of John Adams Way, an inner relief road opened in 1978 (*see* p 70). Boston's through traffic formerly all ran up London Road, the High Street, over the Town Bridge, up the narrow Strait Bargate and then Wide Bargate, resulting in hopeless congestion. Something had to be done but the new road, although it certainly speeded up traffic in the short term, created a whole new set of problems and is now seen as a major blight on the town.

First of all, the relief road divided the east side of the town, that part along Maud Foster Drain, from the centre, splitting many roads in the process. This area declined noticeably following the opening of the new road and the two halves of Main Ridge provide an instructive comparison, as does the High Street, where the southern part was, for many years, a neglected backwater. The road damaged the setting of many listed buildings such as the Unitarian Chapel and runs close to the rear of the important group of buildings on South Street including those in Spain Lane, and the Guildhall and Fydell House. Finally, it was directly responsible for the destruction of a number of worthwhile buildings, especially in the High Street where a swathe was cut through, resulting in the loss of the Lord Nelson, illustrated in the artist John Piper's 1940 *Architectural Review* article 'Fully Licensed' as a fine example of an English pub,[55] and other 18th-century and earlier structures. Other areas particularly badly affected were some of the streets to the east of Pen Street and the approach to Bargate Bridge. The new road did not even bring the hoped-for benefits as it soon became clogged with traffic with conditions approaching gridlock in rush hour. It became such an issue that the Boston Bypass Independents, a group of independents standing on a platform of the need for a bypass, won control of the Council in 2007 and retained it until most lost their seats in the 2011 local election.

The roads to the west of the town centre also became increasingly congested. All the houses on the south side of Liquorpond Street west of the relief road were demolished for road widening and the building of a retail park on land south of the Sleaford Road level crossing and a large supermarket to the north of it have further increased traffic levels. The route of the rail line southwards from Boston was used for a new road linking the town with the A17 which took the traffic away from the southern part of the High Street and London Road but also took much of the life out of it as well.

The development of Pescod Square by Centros (architects: Building Design Partnership), opened in 2004, running around the back of the existing shopping area and linking up the Market Place with Wide Bargate, has provided the large shop units that multiple retailers desire without detracting from the tight-knit fabric of the town centre. Although a little anonymous in appearance, it is of the right scale and has given the town an open-air pedestrian link. It takes its name from the much restored and relocated Pescod Hall that forms its focal point (*see* Fig 14).

But despite these changes and the inevitable clutter associated with catering for traffic (Figs 90 and 91), the centre of Boston is, on the whole remarkably intact. The town is fortunate in having two great market places, both lined with such a rich variety of buildings that have changed little in the last 100 years. It retains its medieval street pattern that is still clearly visible. The changes have occurred behind the main thoroughfares and even a development such as Pescod Square has been fitted in with only minor impact on the principal shopping streets.

In this context, it is interesting to look back at an often surprisingly prescient forecast of the future, *'Boston in 2000 AD. What the "Fenland Port" will be like a hundred years hence'*, written in 1900 by Silas Penny, a young journalist evidently heavily influenced by the writings of H G Wells. He envisaged a world where 'instead of a dozen drapers and a score of grocers we shall be served by elephantine Emporia – one perhaps in the Market Place (where no longer a market will be held) ... and others on the outskirts'. As for getting about, 'lifts, moving ways and revolving staircases will be at the service of the hustling pedestrian' and 'along the glassy streets of our town and the softly humming motors will glide, and in the air graceful areoplanes [sic] will wheel and pironette [sic] around the pinnacles of the "Stump"'.[56] The out of town superstores arrived but the market thrives and, while Boston is beset by traffic, it perhaps fortunately does not have aircraft flitting about the tower of St Botolph's.

Figures 90 and 91
The Red Cow and its neighbouring buildings mainly date from the 18th century and help to give Wide Bargate much of its character. Two contrasting photographs, one taken on 5 June 1942 and the other in 2004, highlight how much more cluttered streets have become in the past 70 years with railings and traffic lights.
[OP19509; DP165419]

The historic core of Boston

The architectural writer Gordon Cullen coined the word 'townscape' in the 1950s to describe the effect of constantly changing vistas of varied buildings on the observer. Boston, in its Market Place, Wide Bargate and South Street, is almost an object lesson in townscape, with buildings of many different periods and styles coming together to form a harmonious whole. The contrast in scale from the broad expanse of the Market Place to the narrow South Street and Strait Bargate, moving from the open space of one to the enclosure of the other two streets is echoed in the narrow medieval lanes that run into its east side. So too is the way in which the open quaysides of the Haven with their views up and down stream and across to the jumbled masses of the buildings on the High Street, contrast with the enclosure of the large granaries and warehouses on South Street. The two areas that form the core of the medieval town are best dealt with in spatial terms rather than chronologically.

The Market Place

Looking south-east across the Market Place, the overall picture has changed little in the past 100 years and most of what can be seen is of the late 18th or early 19th centuries (Fig 92). The space is best explored by imagining oneself outside St Botolph's by the statute of Herbert Ingram (proprietor of *the Illustrated London News*) by Alexander Munro, erected in 1862, which forms a focal point in front of the church, a view immortalised by generations of printmakers and postcard publishers. This is the commercial heart of Boston. Lloyd's Bank, a splendid ashlar-fronted classical building of 1864, was built for William Garfitt & Claypon, bankers who had formerly operated from the great Georgian houses of the High Street (Fig 93). To the left, the view is stopped by the imposing stone premises of the Stamford, Spalding and Boston Joint Stock Banking Co, which was designed by Lockwood & Mawson, a connection explicable as William Mawson was the son-in-law of James Thomas, one of the bank's directors. Built between 1875 and 1876 in Gothic style, the building has lost its mansard roof but remains as Barclay's Bank today (Fig 94). Around the corner, the Market Place diminishes noticeably in width, enhancing the sense of enclosure. On the west side is No 60, once forming part of a larger building, distinguished by Venetian windows at first-floor level. Now the Carphone Warehouse, it has a

An aerial view of the Market Place, looking northwards. The preserved medieval street pattern of the lanes bordered by the Barditch is evident on the right. [28410/111]

Figure 92
A view of the Market Place in the 1870s. No 1 Market Place, designed by Bellamy & Hardy for J Morton in 1861, is in the centre. On the right is the celebrated Five Lamps, 1842–7.
[OP10680]

Figure 93
Lloyd's Bank, built for William Garfit & Claypon in 1864.
[DP160489]

Figure 94 (opposite, top)
Barclays Bank, (Lockwood & Mawson, 1875–6), built as the Stamford, Spalding and Boston Bank.
[DP161458]

Figure 95 (opposite, bottom)
NatWest Bank (Charles Gribble, 1892), built as the National Provincial Bank. The building was extended to the south, and the entrance relocated, in the 20th century.
[With the permission of Lincolnshire Archives]

steep pitched roof and long wing to the rear suggesting that, behind the late 18th-century façade, it may be a much earlier timber-framed building.

Marking the corner of Strait Bargate, is one of those buildings that effortlessly forms a local landmark, No 1 Market Place, the tall four-storey shop of F Hinds. This was designed in 1866 by a prominent firm of Lincoln architects, Bellamy & Hardy, for J Morton as a bookshop. Its height and elaborate use of red-brick dressings to complement the yellow brick used elsewhere in its façade are typical of the way in which 19th-century shopkeepers used architecture to make a statement, to draw attention to their businesses. In complete contrast are the adjoining 18th-century No 2 Market Place and Nos 3–4a Petticoat Lane, which have their origins in the 17th century. The painted brick frontages and lower eaves levels provide variety as do the roof materials with both slate and unusual green pantiles employed. The dentilled eaves in Petticoat Lane are a decorative feature much used in Boston between about 1780 and 1830.

On the corner of Petticoat Lane is Marks & Spencer (*see* p 73). It is followed by three Victorian buildings all contrasting in both height and style, which punctuate the east side and set off the much more demure stuccoed buildings on the west. The first is the NatWest Bank, a sober affair, the northern three bays designed by a London architect, Charles Gribble, for the National Provincial Bank in 1892, and the present entrance added later and almost imperceptibly to the south (Fig 95). Next door at No 13, Poundstretcher's shop hides one of Boston's best-kept secrets. The clue is in the frontage (Fig 96). The original building, which is in a broadly Tudor style, its mullion and transom windows topped with hoodmoulds, was designed as a chemist's shop by Charles Kirk of Sleaford, probably in the 1870s (Fig 97). Converted into the Scala Cinema in 1914, it has a large inserted window with a deeply projecting cornice above it running right across the first floor. Inside, the first-floor foyer still retains much elaborate plasterwork and a barrel-vaulted roof. This leads into the large red-brick cinema building put up behind the original Victorian building. Both the circle and the stalls survive above the current shop premises and the auditorium, disused since the 1950s, retains a wealth of mouldings and decoration (Fig 98). No 15, the Nationwide Building Society is the most exuberant building on the east side. It was built about 1880 as premises for the draper's, Small's (Fig 99). At four storeys, it is tall, its height emphasised by three gables on the top floor and the way in which Gothic windows are grouped in threes under broad arches.

The shop is separated from its neighbours on each side by narrow alleys and the architect, Samuel Sherwin, ingeniously splayed the corners to admit more light. This, combined with the bright red-brick and stone dressings, all helps to make the building stand out.

By comparison, the other buildings on this side of the Market Place are much quieter, mostly with painted or rendered façades of the early 19th century. But there is more to some of them than meets the eye. A glance at the passage on the left side of No 19, currently Savers, reveals a timber post and the building which appears to date from the 18th century is in fact a timber-framed structure with its origins in the late 15th century (*see* Fig 101). The late Victorian fronts of the buildings either side of No 19 hide early 18th-century buildings behind. Three more buildings – No 24, The Norwich & Peterborough Building Society, No 27–8 Halifax and No 29 Specsavers have medieval fabric hidden within them. At Nos 27–8 the timber posts supporting the jettied front are still visible through the shop windows. Although it is not immediately obvious, quite a few ancient buildings remain in the heart of the town overlaying the medieval street layout of Boston, and still fulfilling the important commercial role that they have played for over 500 years. Subsequent periods have brought changes that are reflected in them, often in attractive details such as the Regency shopfront of Nos 27–8 with its bow windows (Fig 100).

What is so striking about the Market Place is how well it works as a space. Boston, on Wednesday and Saturday market days is still a bustling place, thronged with shoppers. The shops, cafes and pubs are packed just as they would have been a hundred or two hundred years ago. Unlike many market towns in East Anglia where the market has become something of a token event, Boston's still has vitality to it, exemplified in the entertainment provided by the street auction in Wide Bargate. So large a space can easily become sterile when not filled with market stalls and for many years, Boston's Market Place suffered by being used for heavy through traffic and then for car parking. It was a sea of dull asphalt but the Council's repaving scheme (Fig 101), with its employment of grey setts has improved the view and importantly has retained the distinction between pavement and roadway, the removal of which has in some towns introduced a note of bland uniformity.

Rather than taking stalls in the Market Place itself, the many corn merchants trading from Boston tended to occupy booths on market days located

Figure 96
No 13 Market Place today, occupied by Poundstretcher. The large window inserted in 1914 for the conversion to the Scala Cinema evident above the fascia.
[John Minnis]

Figure 97 (above)
No 13 Market Place, designed by Charles Kirk as
a chemist's shop.
[With the permission of Lincolnshire Archives]

Figure 98 (above, right)
The interior of the Scala Cinema showing the
balcony and surviving fibrous plaster decoration.
[John Minnis]

in mobile huts or the medieval lanes running off the Market Place. There are still some of these to be seen in Grant's Lane on the side of No 24. There was also much business carried out in the numerous pubs around the Market Place and the lanes leading off it. The Still (*see* Fig 101), old enough to give its name to the lane in which it stands, has recently closed and the last one remaining is The Stump and Candle (formerly the Rum Puncheon) of early 18th-century origin. The two coaching inns, the Red Lion in Strait Bargate and the Peacock & Royal, were both replaced by commercial development, the former in 1963 and the latter, an ancient inn with a later façade that was a great adornment to the Market Place, was demolished in 1966. In its place was built the present Boots store, an especially bland structure, intended with its pitched roof, brick walls and small windows to fit in to its setting but, as so often happened with this sort of half-hearted approach in historic towns in the 1970s, completely failing to do so and proving a very poor substitute for its predecessor. The butcher's nearby

Figure 99 (left)
The former Small's draper's store at No 15 Market Place.
[DP165386]

Figure 100 (above)
A Georgian front hides medieval timber-framing behind at Nos 27–8 Market Place. The Regency shopfront is one of the best in Boston.
[DP165391]

replaced another attractive building in the 1960s but it at least had the courage of its convictions, employing what was then an up-to-date style: the well-maintained shopfront with its small tiles has begun to acquire something of a period charm.

Fortunately, this sort of thing was rare in the Market Place and the west side is completely intact. It is quite different in character to the east side, having

Figure 101
The newly replaced lamp and the repaving of the
Market Place are clearly seen here. In the background
is No 19 Savers, which is at its core a late 15th-century
timber-framed building – an ancient timber post is
visible in the alley on its left. To the right, the Still, closed
shortly before this photograph was taken in 2014, was
once one of the many pubs serving marketgoers.
[DP165384]

much more of a civic character with four substantial elements of it being
developed by Boston Corporation. The scale is much more uniform, the
buildings being a generally consistent height, with none of the shopkeepers'
extravagances seen on the opposite side. It is a long way from being monotonous
and it achieves a grandeur befitting Boston's position as the largest town in
Lincolnshire at the beginning of the 19th century.

Starting at the south end, a pair of houses of 1777 (now the Waterfront pub)
set the scale, which is briefly broken by the gable of an intriguing building,
No 34 (now incorporated into the pub). It managed to combine the functions of
a theatre and warehouse by operating as a theatre during a short spring season
and a warehouse for the remainder of the year. Its use as a theatre ended in
1806. Nos 32–4 were all built by the Corporation. From this point, the Market
Place widens out, giving an appropriately grand setting to Corporation (later
Exchange) Buildings (*see* p 31), occupying much of the west side, right up to the
Town Bridge (Fig 102).

The building of the new Town Bridge over the River Witham in 1807 left a
space to the north of the bridge, formerly occupied by the approach road to its

Figure 102
Corporation Buildings, built in 1770 by the Corporation, has had many alterations to the ground floor but the basic form of the building, with its palace front, is still evident.
[DP161464]

predecessor. In 1812, the Corporation asked Robert Atkinson, a prominent country house architect responsible for, among many other houses, Abbotsford, Melrose, Roxburghshire (home of Sir Walter Scott) and Deepdene, near Dorking, Surrey (built for Thomas Hope), to draw up plans for an assembly room and a fish market to be built on the site. Atkinson did not execute his designs but still charged for his plans. The new Fish Market, replacing that in Corporation Buildings which was converted to municipal offices, was built in 1816 under the supervision of John Farnsworth, who was the resident engineer for the works under the Boston Harbour Act. The Butter Cross Assembly Rooms in the Market Place had been built in 1732 and its replacement was now overdue. The new Assembly Rooms (Fig 103), which had an open Butter Market underneath them, were built from 1819 to 1822, the work being supervised by Jeptha Pacey, the surveyor to the Corporation and a major landlord (largely of slum property) in the town. The open space below was later filled in and converted to shops. To what extent the design of the building as constructed is attributable to Atkinson or to Pacey is unknown in the absence of surviving contemporary drawings.[57]

Figure 103
The Assembly Rooms (work supervised by Jepha Pacey, 1819–22).
[DP161460]

Both Corporation Buildings and the Assembly Rooms, despite their prominent location, their importance to the town and their architectural quality have been neglected in recent years, although some renovation of the Assembly Rooms has taken place.

The fourth piece of municipal enterprise in the Market Place is a terrace of six shops between the Assembly Rooms and St Botolph's Church. Completed in 1820, the terrace (Nos 45–50) has a convex façade of plain appearance that has had its brickwork painted for many years (Fig 104). It is one of the earliest examples in England of what would later become known as a shopping parade with access to the living quarters above the shops being by stairways from the rear. The role of a Corporation in instigating development of commercial property as a municipal improvement, other than with market halls, was relatively rare at this time. Much of the west side of the Market Place is the result of planned development by a public body but not the sort of gesture which we associate with the term today – there is nothing in the way of grand axial vistas

or tightly controlled formality here – just the sort of ad hoc development that fits well into a market place that had grown up over the centuries. Boston is all the better for it. The curve of the façade injects another element that enlivens the complex form of the Market Place. The block in which these shops stand may originally have been part of the open market place. As with many markets, stalls became semi-permanent and eventually shops were built on their site, their small plots contrasting with the deep burgage plots to be found around the original boundaries of the market.

South Street and South Square

Continuing southwards from the Market Place, this is the area that most fully evokes Boston's maritime past. Coming from the great open space of the Market Place, the narrowness of the street is immediately apparent and would have been even more marked before two of the warehouses on the west side and the butcher's shop on the east were demolished for road widening in the 1960s. The demolitions have led to the riverscape being more exposed to the road with fine views looking back up to the Town Bridge and St Botolph's tower as the road curves, following the line of the Haven. Before, the effect might have been more like a canyon with tall warehouses lining both sides of the road.

The quayside was rebuilt by John Rennie in 1812 and the stone edging of the walls and steps up the quay are clearly evident as are, at low tide, the remains of timber jetties. The most serious loss was the London Warehouse on Packhouse Quay, built by the Corporation in 1817: its much taller twin may still be seen on Doughty Quay on the west bank of the Haven. The view opened up by its demise is that of the backs of the shops on the High Street, an extraordinary mixture of shapes and building materials as extension followed extension – the antithesis of planning – formed over a long period of time although the last 50 years have made no significant contribution. F L Griggs made some evocative sketches of the riverscape for *Highways and Byways in Lincolnshire*.

The first building on the east side is Shodfriars Hall (Fig 105). This was a major 15th-century timber-framed building with some conjectural evidence linking it to the Guild of Corpus Christi. The building survived into the second

Figure 104
The Market Place, showing the setting of St Botolph's and, on the left, part of the terrace of shops built by the Corporation in 1820.
[DP151433]

93

Figure 105
Shodfriars Hall.
[DP161082]

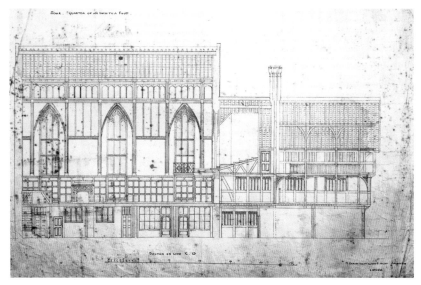

Figure 106
Plans prepared by George Gilbert Scott Jnr and John
Oldrid Scott for the reconstruction of Shodfriars Hall.
[With the permission of Lincolnshire Archives]

Figure 107
No 10 South Street.
[DP161488]

half of the 19th century by which time it had attracted antiquarian interest, Pishey Thompson including a drawing of it in his *History of Boston*. It was acquired by Samuel Sherwin who turned it into a public hall and Conservative Club. Although often acting as an architect himself, he realised that the work required a specialist in restoration and he went to George Gilbert Scott Jnr and John Oldrid Scott (Fig 106).

Less obvious was the form the restoration took. At first sight, the timber-framed front portion, with its four storeys, twin gables and overly black and white treatment, looks far too good to be true, and to some extent it is. *Boston Society* referred to it in 1900 as being 'a spurious imitation'. But it is not a 19th-century fabrication as many writers have alleged. Substantial parts of the timbers in the lower part of the building are original, as shown on Scott's drawings which are preserved in the Lincolnshire Archives. Much of the work was quite scholarly and 17th-century panelling remains on the first floor as does Scott's original paint scheme on the top floor. The reconstruction of the front portion is in itself a dramatic example of 19th -century Tudor revival, comparable to the work that John Douglas and others were undertaking in Chester. It is the addition at the rear that catches the eye today and demonstrates some highly original treatment. The hall is immensely tall with a very steeply pitched roof, clad in red and white brick, used decoratively to form panels, in a style that was inspired by Flemish or possibly Baltic originals. Was this a conscious reference to Boston's Hanseatic past? Contemporary reports describe the building to be in the Flemish style. Crow-stepped gables and tall, narrow windows in an unlikely and distinctly foreign looking Perpendicular complete the sense of being somewhere far from Lincolnshire.

The same influences are brought to bear just two doors down at No 10 which has a tall gabled front that looks as though it has been plucked straight out of a northern European city (Fig 107). The vertical emphasis with tall narrow Gothic windows is heightened by the use of thin shafts of triangular profile running up to the gable, all designed to take our eyes upwards. Tracery in the tympana above the windows owes much to Dutch examples. The building is clearly intended to be read with Shodfriars Hall but its designer remains unknown, as does its date of construction. It was sufficiently convincing to stand in, along with other buildings in the town, for the Netherlands in the 1942 Powell & Pressburger film *One of our Aircraft is Missing*. A walk along the alley

at its side, leading to the Ship Tavern (Fig 108), reveals some medieval masonry and a couple of blocked openings of similar date (*see* Fig 10). These, together with an arcade in its basement, are probably fragments of the buildings of the Dominicans or Black Friars. The building was originally the Shodfriars Club, formed 1875, and later housed the billiards, reading and card rooms of the Boston Club, which moved here in 1895.

More ancient fabric is to be seen within the large, apparently late Georgian Pilgrim House, the premises of the wine and spirit merchants, Ridlington's, for many years. It had been the London Tavern until taken over by James Ridlington about 1861. Within, there is evidence of timber-framing dating back to 1668. The Custom House of 1725 (Fig 109) and more elegant 18th- and early 19th-century buildings follow, juxtaposed with the tall former Britannia Oil Mill of 1856, later used as a seed warehouse, and now converted to apartments as

Figure 108 (above, left)
The Ship Tavern. An early 19th-century pub, typical of many that once served the market and the quays.
[DP160498]

Figure 109 (above)
The Custom House (1725).
[DP161490]

Pilgrim Mansions. These buildings combine to make probably the most satisfying group in Boston, varying tremendously in date, style, size and materials yet all fitting together to provide real drama either seen close to or from the Town Bridge.

Up Spain Lane to the east is Nos 3–9, a terrace of small early 18th-century houses designed as a group with those in the centre brought forward and embellished with a pediment, a clear attempt at a formal composition reminiscent on a small scale of the palace front that was then the fashion in places such as Bath, although one's appreciation of the design is impaired by the narrow width of the street (Fig 110). Then the Blackfriars Theatre, in the medieval building once forming part of Blackfriars (*see* p 10 and p 15), stands on the corner of Spain Court, with two rows of mid-18th-century cottages facing each other on the east and west sides of the Court (Fig 111). All these buildings are owned by the Boston Preservation Trust, which purchased them in 1935 as part of its acquisition of Fydell House in a pioneering move to preserve minor Georgian houses, something very rare at the time. Consequently, they have retained the majority of their historic features, unlike many of the smaller Georgian houses in the town.

Continuing down South Street, the St Mary's Guildhall (*see* Fig 5) catches the eye. The gabled frontage to South Street, with its vast traceried west window, is perhaps easily mistaken for a religious building: indeed, the more modest ground floor of the building did once function as a chapel for the guild but the grand window above lit a great hall. The true extent of the building can only be appreciated when one looks down the side of the building, along Beadsman's Lane – the Guildhall is an extraordinarily long and narrow building which corresponds to the ancient boundaries of the burgage plot on which it was built around 1390. Much of the brickwork is original, making it some of the earliest in England (at least since Roman times).

The warehouses along the west side of the road provide Boston with much of its identity as a port. Now that most of the similar structures at Wisbech have been destroyed, they form one of the best groups of 18th-century warehouses in England. They date from the greatly increased grain trade following the draining of the fens and the improvement in navigation after the opening in 1766 of the Grand Sluice. Neil Wright has suggested that much of the Dominican friary was taken over for use as warehousing after the Dissolution which has led to the

Figure 110
No 3–9 Spain Lane, a formal composition of modest early 18th-century houses.
[DP161497]

Figure 111
Cottages on the east side of Spain Court face a matching terrace on the west side of a small square.
[John Minnis]

Figure 112
Lincoln's warehouse, now the Sam Newsom Music
Centre, mid-18th century and later.
[John Minnis]

survival of the Blackfriars building, now used as a theatre, and of the fragments in Pilgrim House and No 10 South Street.[58] Other elements of the friary survived in buildings between Spain Lane and Custom House Lane until a great fire destroyed the whole block in 1844.

The 18th-century warehouses were built of brick with timber floors and no attempt at fireproofing. The first we encounter, Lincoln's warehouse, was sold in 1976 to the County Council and has been re-used as the Sam Newsom Music Centre, one of the earliest examples of adaptive re-use in the town (Fig 112). It was built in three phases. The earliest is that facing South Street built in the mid-18th century. Two wings were added, filling the space between the first stage and the Haven in the latter part of the century – the break in the brickwork is still evident on the north elevation. Finally the space between the wings was infilled by 1811.[59]

Then we have another of those shifts in width that makes Boston's townscape so interesting. South Street suddenly widens out to form South Square. It has lost some of its impact with the demolition of Sheath's Granary,

Figure 113
A view up the Haven on 4 June 1942, showing the rear
of the group of 18th-century warehouses on South
Street and South Square with the London Warehouse of
1817 on Packhouse Quay visible just beyond them.
[OP19544]

which, although opening up new views of the High Street and the Doughty Quay
Public warehouse on the west bank (Figs 113 and 114) , has removed its sense
of enclosure with the proximity of John Adams Way to the south only making
things worse. But it is still a fine space with the view to the north blocked by No
9 South Square, a Georgian house that was incorporated into the Magnet
Tavern. Until 1810, South Square was still one of the premier residential areas of
Boston with few warehouses south of Custom House Lane. By far the most
impressive building in it, placed next to the Guildhall, is Fydell House (*see* Fig
21), set well back from the road behind handsome iron railings. Although it has
been suggested that its façade bears the mark of a provincial architect in the
unsophisticated way in which so many different elements are packed together in
the entrance bay, the overall effect is appropriately grand.

Two large grain warehouses block the view to the Haven. One, now
converted to apartments as Haven Hall, was built by Thomas Fydell in 1810 on
the site of Gysor's Hall, a merchant's house of the early 11th century that was
later turned into a warehouse. Some medieval masonry was salvaged from
Gysor's Hall and forms part of the ground floor of the present building. The
Middle Warehouse (now Riverside Lodge) comprises a pair of granaries running

Figure 114
Taken on 20 July 1929 from a little to the south of
Figure 113, this is looking east to Doughty Quay with
the Public Warehouse of c 1820 prominent just below
the tower of St Botolph's.
[BB67/09316]

down to the river, linked by a covered passage, an arrangement evident from the roof structure (Fig 115). It has the hip-and-gablet roofs seen in similar warehouses at Wisbech. On the east side stand two houses that, though they are not as striking as Fydell House, reflect the tradition of the merchant families of Boston living close to the river and to their businesses. No 4 Rice House was built by the merchant Charles Rice (c 1783–1843) between 1818 when he acquired the site and 1824, when the house was described as 'lately erected' (Fig 116). Now offices, it remained in the hands of his descendants until 1952. The plain façade is enlivened by a handsome open pediment over the door and its most extraordinary feature is its remarkably deep eaves: eaves could be deep in Regency times but this is exceptional. Inside, it has characteristic Regency door frames with flutes terminating in blocks on the corners and an elegant staircase. No 5 to its south remained a private house until 1961 and probably dates from the early to mid-18th century. It too was in the hands of some of Boston's notable families: Richard Fydell owned it in 1766 and in 1823 it was bought by John Oldrid who lived there until his death in 1849. White-painted stucco and black-painted dressings contrast with the sober brickwork of Rice House.

Figure 115 (above, left)
The surviving warehouse group in South Square. On the left is the Middle Warehouse (now Riverside Lodge) and on the right, Haven Hall, on the site of Gysor's Hall.
[John Minnis]

Figure 116 (above)
No 4 Rice House with its extraordinarily deep eaves.
[John Minnis]

Figure 117
Nos 6–7 South Square, c 1798–9, looking across
John Adams Way.
[DP161490]

At this point, John Adams Way intervenes but there are two further houses in South Square, Nos 6 and 7, on the far side of it (Fig 117). They comprise a matching pair of houses that are probably those recorded in the account book of the architect Francis Carter of London as two new houses built for Thomas Fydell between 1798 and 1799. Both houses are very much in the local style with red-brick façades, dentilled eaves cornices and (originally) doorways at the side with surrounds similar to those installed by John Watson in the terrace at Witham Place about the same time. No 7 retains its side entrance but No 6 has had a large addition to the north that has subsequently undergone considerable alteration, including the provision of a splendid first-floor bay window giving views up and down the Haven.

7

Boston: The present day

Clive Fletcher and Mary Anderson

To picture Boston as a key hub in an international transport superhighway requires a feat of imagination, and yet this is what it was in the medieval period. Water-borne travel was quite simply the fastest route to most places, either across the seas, as inshore 'hops' between ports, or as part of the inland waterways network that linked the town to the Midlands and the North. By contrast, the road network was slow and unreliable. The eventual silting of the Haven deprived Boston of much of this advantage, while the increase in intercontinental trade and the expansion of Bristol and Liverpool signalled an economic reorientation to the west, away from the historic associations between Eastern England and Northern Europe.

Today Boston's remoteness is part of its charm, and has in some respects saved it from becoming one of the identikit towns lamented in the media. This very self-reliance has no doubt contributed to it being assessed as one of the most resilient of Lincolnshire towns during the recent economic crisis. There is a new vitality and confidence detectable in Boston, and its fascinating heritage is increasingly seen as a key to its future.

Regeneration

Regeneration through investment in the historic environment has a long history in the town, and many buildings owe their survival to the timely offer of grant aid for urgent repairs. These buildings, which include the warehouses that line the Haven, are now host to an array of small businesses, homes and community activities, as well as forming the townscape that is so much valued for its character.

Most recently, leadership from both the County and Borough Councils resulted in a reappraisal of the historic Market Place and an investment of £2.4m in its rejuvenation. This ambitious public realm project has few equals nationally in terms of quality or extent. Like many public spaces, the Market Place had been subject to years of piecemeal repairs, with no clear strategic management beyond the day to day practicalities of maintaining the market and providing car parking.

Extensive historical research revealed that far from always being a single open space, the Market Place was punctuated by buildings such as the Butter Market (which contained the earlier assembly room for the town) and post-

The Five Lamps and the repaved Market Place. [DP172405]

medieval encroachments, while historic photographs showed it to have had a largely homogenous surface. Also evident in these photographs is the lost Five Lamps, which had lit the space until replaced by a more modern structure in the 1930s, before it too was transplanted to a site in Liquorpond Street on the edge of town.

During field archaeological field evaluations both basalt and pink granite setts were found beneath the modern surface of the Market Place – both of which are still found throughout the East Midlands and in the Low Countries, as for example in Ghent's Korenmakt. For reasons of availability, however, York stone was eventually chosen for the setts that cover the square, and (as would almost certainly have been the case in the 19th century), used as paving slabs around the periphery. The effect, visually, is stunning, and has improved the appearance of the Market Place and the setting of St Botolph's beyond measure.

The repaving also presented an opportunity to assess the town's nationally important buried archaeology, which due to the waterlogged nature of the land and the concerted attempts to lay down materials to increase surface levels rather than reduce them are exceptionally well preserved. A hugely popular community archaeology project uncovered the foundations of a number of the lost structures in the Market Place, and a rich sequence of archaeological deposits, while more portable artefacts were displayed in the Guildhall Museum.

The re-presentation of the Market Place considers the 'public realm' in its fullest sense, and the repaving is just part of a wider partnership project with shopkeepers around the Market Place to reinstate lost architectural details to its many fine buildings.

The Five Lamps

Part of the scheme included a recreation of the lamp standard that had previously stood in the Market Place in the 19th and early 20th centuries. It was (as the name suggests) a distinctive design bearing five lanterns: the largest, dating from 1842, on the top and four slightly smaller ones added in 1847 on projecting bars beneath it. The main column was quite ornate and had a large base around which the townsfolk used to sit and gather for a chat.

There are no drawings available of this earlier centrepiece but many photographs show the structure, and these were studied in great detail to enable a replica lamp to be made. This was cast in Bristol by specialist iron founders and re-erected in Boston in July 2013 on a new circular granite base. The only difference is that the new lamps are electrically operated rather than gas lit. The surprising aspect of this lamp is its scale – at over 8m tall and 3m in diameter, it 'furnishes' the square in a way a smaller lantern could not.

European migration

The economy and community of Boston has recently seen quite significant change as large numbers of people from EU member states have settled in the town. This has brought opportunities as well as challenges for the historic environment, from those presented by a demand for more rented properties and flats, resulting in the multiple occupancy of many of the larger Georgian houses, to the vibrant re-use of historic commercial buildings for the shops, restaurants and other businesses that have opened. The revived practice of 'living above the shop', has also heralded a renewed vitality around the Market Place, as once vacant upper floors return to full use, while there is also an increased interest locally in the history of Boston and its links with its former Baltic trading partners.

Waterways

Boston's proximity to water is again being turned to its advantage, in the form of water-borne tourism. The re-establishment of Boston as a hub for boat traffic is being realised by the Fenlands Waterways Link, which is the most ambitious canal building initiative for over a century. It allows a 'three cathedrals' boating circuit though Peterborough, Ely and Lincoln taking in the Rivers Nene, Great Ouse, Welland and Witham, and through the Fossdyke further still onto the Trent system.

The project is closely associated with a flood alleviation scheme, the Boston Barrier, which will restrict the tidal range of the River Witham, allowing boat traffic to navigate through the town at all phases of the tide, something hitherto impossible. A key element of the project, a new lock between the South Forty-Foot Drain and the River Witham at the Black Sluice has already been completed.

Although the rotting hulks and mud banks are unquestionably an evocative expression of Boston's maritime heritage, the recent flooding in the town demonstrates the need for protection against the tidal surges that cause it. The partial loss of the tidal aspect of the river's character must therefore be balanced against the needs of Boston's future, and the benefits above and beyond flood protection are seen as a welcome dividend to the economy of the town.

The rescue of No 116 High Street

This substantial early 18th-century house was converted into Lincolnshire's first bank in 1754 by William Garfitt, to serve the Georgian boom town (Fig 118 and *see* Fig 22). Listed at Grade II*, it was latterly used as a potato merchant's premises before being abandoned in the 1990s to become increasingly derelict. The theft of lead from all of the roofs led to saturation and extensive rot, and when this was discovered, a complex support scaffold had to be installed inside the building to prevent collapse.

Without such statutory interventions by the Borough Council and the eventual compulsory purchase from the absentee owner, it would almost certainly have been lost. Instead, the building was saved, and an exemplary

Figure 118
No 116 High Street from the rear, showing the extensive restoration that has taken place, together with the creation of a garden for community use.
[DP160255]

restoration undertaken by the Heritage Trust for Lincolnshire using grants from English Heritage, the Heritage Lottery Fund, Architectural Heritage Fund, Lincolnshire County Council, European Regional Development Fund, John Paul Getty Jnr Trust and the Pilgrim Trust.

Although near the centre of the historic town, the property had the remains of a large garden area which originally extended eastwards as far as the banks of the Haven. Much of this garden area had in part been swallowed up by late 19th-century terraces, and the remainder concreted over and covered in sheds. The sheds, concrete and some poor 20th-century extensions were cleared away, the house carefully repaired, and the fine bow window restored to the garden front.

In the grounds a row of neat red-brick office/workshop units were constructed facing the reinstated garden area, with a glazed canopy over a terrace. The site is now back in use, and the effect this has had on the appearance of the High Street has been transformative.

St Botolph's footbridge

The totemic view from the town bridge to St Botolph's tower has been greatly enhanced by the construction of a modern bowstring bridge across the river (Fig 119), which elegantly paraphrases the 19th-century railway bridge at the Grand Sluice. It was chosen by public vote from three concept designs by local architects Neil Dowlman Ltd. The winning scheme was developed and funded by Lincolnshire County Council engineers, with specialist bridge builder Britcon, and made off site before being craned into position in February 2014. With its shallower extended slope it has proved to be well used and popular.

The future

At the time of writing, the quality of Boston, both past and present, is not widely acknowledged or appreciated. Ambitious projects have solved a range of problems, and more are in development, but there remain significant barriers to it achieving its full potential.

Figure 119
The footbridge over the River Witham, designed by
Neil Dowlman Ltd and installed in 2014.
[DP151270]

The most harmful of these are the effects of traffic and the legacy of efforts to accommodate it. The thinking implicit in Sir Colin Buchanan's influential 1963 report, *Traffic in Towns*, is all too well illustrated by the effects of John Adams Way, and, until this is tamed, significant parts of the town will be blighted by proximity to it and severed from the town centre. There are popular and understandable calls for the town to be bypassed, but much could be done to improve matters by modifying the existing road. The implementation, appropriately, of *woonerf* principles of Dutch street design would deliver a less engineered, more pedestrian friendly environment. This could be achieved incrementally using the County Council's own innovative *Streetscape Design Manual*, and would not require the vast sums the construction of a new road would involve.

The many shopkeepers and homeowners also have a critical part to play, as Boston not only impresses through its magnificent set pieces, but also by the huge collection of Georgian, Victorian and the high-quality 20th-century buildings that line its streets and public spaces (Fig 120). As always, informed stewardship will be the key to fostering the confidence to invest in these assets, and the Borough Council's role in this will continue to be of critical importance.

Figure 120
Intricate detail in a bay window of an early
20th-century house in Tawney Street. It is an example
of the decorative work that adds character to a
neighbourhood and is so often swept away, to be
replaced by mass-produced uPVC components.
[John Minnis]

The houses that surround Central Park are a testament to the value of this in their retention of the ornate windows and doors that contribute so much to their character. The wider application of planning controls to achieve the same in other residential streets would therefore merit due consideration.

The momentum created by strong leadership from the Borough and County Councils has improved prospects for further good works, as the value of Boston's conserved heritage is revealed, but at publication the future of the vacant Sessions House remains in doubt. However, public ownership should enable its sympathetic re-use and the contribution a vibrant new function could make to the life and economy of Boston would be inestimable.

A vision for the future of Boston, tantalisingly within reach, is as a town firmly established on the mainstream tourist map of England, with an economy not only resilient, but again prosperous due to its historic and continuing relationship with the water and the land, and for its unique character. For the visitor, it must surely take its place as one of the emblems of England's rich maritime and urban heritage and demonstrate the ability for our historic towns to adapt and thrive.

Notes

1 Richardson 1921, 34–42

2 Lambert and Walker 1930, 106

3 Pevsner and Harris 1995, 156

4 Palmer-Brown 1996, 10

5 Anon 2000, 5

6 St Botolph's was situated within Richmond Fee, part of the Honour of Richmond – lands awarded by the king.

7 Dugdale 1686, 46. The original charter is believed to be in the *Registrum Antiqissimum of the Cathedral Church of Lincoln* (*c* 1235).

8 Poole 1951, 80

9 Palmer-Brown 1995, 4

10 Anon 1995, 3

11 Hill 1965, 312

12 Rylatt 2000, 8

13 Clark *et al* 2003, 15

14 Patent Rolls 1898, 322

15 Thompson 1856, 37

16 Ibid, 338

17 Farrer and Travers 2013, 315

18 Pipe Rolls 1894, 5

19 Calendar of Letter-Books 1909

20 Clark *et al* 2003, 4

21 Ibid

22 Anon 1994, 1

23 Ibid and Jordan 2004, 7

24 Rylatt 2000, 8

25 Close Rolls 1904, 105

26 Anon 2000, 3

27 Ibid, 5

28 Rigby 1985, 52

29 Major 1963, 46

30 Nichols 2014, 101

31 Thorne 1989, 5

32 Rylatt 2000, 7

33 Anon 2000, 6

34 Clark *et al* 2003, 42

35 Ibid

36 Clark *et al* 2003, 50

37 Ibid, 43

38 Ibid

39 Ibid, 7

40 Ibid, 43

41 Thompson 1856, 235

42 Named after Lord Hussey, owner of the tower in the early 16th century, and who was executed for treason following his involvement in the Pilgrimage of Grace – at which point his estates were forfeited to the Crown.

43 Smith 1979, 34

44 N R Wright, pers comm, 20 December 2014. *See also* Hall's map of 1741(p 22) and Wood's map of 1829 (p 32) for the location of the possible gatehouse, and Thompson 1856, 205 for an illustration of the complex.

45 Clark 2001

46 Harden 1978, 30

47 Garner 2012

48 Richardson 1921, 39

49 Hewlings 1988

50 *Stamford Mercury* 12 January 1803

51 Deeds to No 33 Wide Bargate, courtesy Neil Wright.

52 www.horrywood.co.uk (accessed 22 July 2014)

53 *Lincolnshire Standard* 16 April 1955

54 Pevsner and Harris 1995, 162

55 Piper 1940, 87–100

56 *Boston Society* 1900, 453–5

57 This account is indebted to Hewlings 1988.

58 Lewis and Wright 1974, 26

59 For the South Street and South Square warehouses *see* Lewis and Wright 1974.

References and further reading

Anon 1994 *Archaeological Watching Brief at 35 Paddock Grove, Boston, Lincolnshire.* Sleaford: Archaeological Project Services

Anon 1995 *Excavations at Red Lion Street, Boston.* Lincoln: Trust for Lincolnshire Archaeology

Anon 2000 *Archaeological Field Evaluation Report: The Haven Cinema Site, South Square, Boston, Lincolnshire.* Lincoln: John Samuels Archaeological Consultants

Anderson and Glenn 2009 *Boston Market Place, Conservation Area Appraisal.* Boston [available at www.boston.gov.uk (accessed 22 July 2015)]

Bagley, G S 1986 *Boston: Its Story and People.* Boston

Calendar of Letter-Books 1909 *Calendar of Letter-Books of the City of London I: 1400–1422, folio clxxvi(b), Aug 1416.* London: HMSO

Close Rolls 1904 *Calendar of the Close Rolls Preserved in the Public Record Office, Edward I:* **3***, 1288–1296.* London: HMSO

Clark, J 2001 *Timber Survey, Pescod Hall Boston.* Sheffield: Field Archaeology Services

Clark, J, Giles K and Nash, A 2003 *Historic Building Investigation: St Mary's Guildhall, Boston, Lincolnshire.* York: Field Archaeology Specialists Ltd

Dugdale, W 1686 *The Baronage of England.* London

Farrer, W and Travers, C T (eds) 2013 *Early Yorkshire Charters Volume 4: The Honour of Richmond, Part One.* Cambridge: Cambridge University Press

Garner A A 2012 *The Grandest House in Town,* 2 edn. Boston: Richard Kay

Gurnham, R 2014 *The Story of Boston.* Stroud: The History Press

Harden, G 1978 *Medieval Boston and its Archaeological Implications.* Sleaford: South Lincolnshire Archaeological Unit

Hewlings, R 1988 'The Public Buildings of Boston 1702–1822'.

Unpublished paper read to the Association of Art Historians, Sheffield, 9 April 1988

Hill, F 1965 *Medieval Lincoln.* Cambridge: Cambridge University Press

Jordan, M 2004 *71 High Street, Boston, Lincolnshire: Archaeological Excavation.* Lincoln: Lindsey Archaeological Services

Lambert, M R & Walker, R 1930 *Boston, Tattershall and Croyland.* Oxford: Blackwell

Lewis, M J T & Wright N R 1974 *Boston as a Port.* Lincoln: Society for Lincolnshire History and Archaeology

Lincolnshire County Council 2008 Streetscape Design Manual [available at www.lincolnshire.gov.uk (accessed 22 June 2015)]

Major, K (ed)1963 *The Registrum Antiquissimum of the Cathedral Church of Lincoln,VII.* Lincoln: The Lincoln Record Society

Nichols, D 2014 *The Growth of the Medieval City From Late Antiquity to the Early Fourteenth Century,* 2 edn. Abingdon: Routledge

Palmer-Brown, C 1995 *3 New Street Boston: An Archaeological Watching Brief and Survey Report.* Lincoln: Pre-Construct Archaeology

Palmer-Brown, C 1996 *Boston Grammar School: Archaeological Evaluation Report.* Lincoln: Pre-Construct Archaeology

Patent Rolls 1898 *Calendar of the Patent Rolls Preserved in the Public Record Office, Edward I: AD 1301–1307.* London: HMSO.

Pevsner, N & Harris J, revised Antram, N 1995 *The Buildings of England: Lincolnshire.* Harmondsworth: Penguin

Pipe Rolls 1894 *The Great Roll of the Pipe for the Eighteenth Year of the Reign of King Henry II: AD 1171–72.* London: The Pipe Roll Society

Piper, J 1940 'Fully Licensed'. *Architectural Review* **87**, 87–100

Poole, A L 1951 *The Oxford History of England: From Domesday Book to Magna Carta, 1087–1216*. London: Oxford University Press

Reports of the Steering Group and Working Groups appointed by the Minister of Transport 1963 *Traffic in Towns – A study of the long term problems of traffic in urban areas* (Buchanan Report). London: HMSO

Richardson, A E 1921 'The Charm of the Country Town V. Boston, Lincolnshire'. *Architectural Review* **49**, 34–42

Rawnsky, W F 1914 *Highways and Byways in Lincolnshire*. London: Macmillan

Rigby, S H 1985 '"Sore Decay" and "Fair Dwellings": Boston and urban decline in the late middle ages'. *Midland History* **10**, 47–61

Rigby, S H 2012 'Medieval Boston: economy, society and administration' in Badham, S & Cockerham, P C (eds) *The Church of St Botolph's, Boston and its Medieval Monuments*. BAR Brit Ser

Rylatt, J 2000 *Archaeological Watching Brief Report: 25 Witham Place, Boston, Lincolnshire*. Lincoln: Pre-Construct Archaeology

Smith, T P 1979 'Hussey Tower, Boston: a late-medieval tower-house of brick'. *Lincolnshire History and Archaeology* **14**

Thompson, P 1856 *The History and Antiquities of Boston*. Boston

Thorne, R 1989 *Excavations on Wormgate Boston, Lincolnshire: Interim Report*. Lincoln: Trust for Lincolnshire Archaeology

Wheeler, W H 1898 *A History of the Fens of South Lincolnshire*, 2 edn, Boston: J M Newcomb

Wright, N R 1982 *Lincolnshire Towns and Industry 1700–1914*. Lincoln: History of Lincolnshire Committee

Wright, N R 1991 *The Book of Boston*. Buckingham: Barracuda Books

Wright, N R 1994 *Boston, A Pictorial History*. Chichester: Phillimore

Wright, N R 1998 *The Railways of Boston*. Boston: Richard Kay

Wright, N R 2005 *Boston: A History and Celebration*. Dinton: Francis Frith

Informed Conservation Series

This popular Historic England series highlights the special character of some of our most important historic areas and the development pressures they are facing. There are over 30 titles in the series, some of which look at whole towns such as Bridport, Coventry and Margate or distinctive urban districts, such as the Jewellery Quarter in Birmingham and Ancoats in Manchester, while others focus on particular building types in a particular place. A few are national in scope focusing, for example, on English school buildings and garden cities.

The purpose of the series is to raise awareness in a non-specialist audience of the interest and importance of aspects of the built heritage of towns and cities undergoing rapid change or large-scale regeneration. A particular feature of each book is a final chapter that focuses on conservation issues, identifying good examples of the re-use of historic buildings and highlighting those assets or areas for which significant challenges remain.

As accessible distillations of more in-depth research, they also provide a useful resource for heritage professionals, tackling, as many of the books do, places and buildings types that have not previously been subjected to investigation from the historic environment perspective. As well as providing a lively and informed discussion of each subject, the books also act as advocacy documents for Historic England and its partners in promoting the management of change in the historic environment.

More information on each of the books in the series and on forthcoming titles, together with links to enable them to be ordered or downloaded is available on the Historic England website.

HistoricEngland.org.uk

Market Place walk

KEY

1   Herbert Ingram
    Monument

2   Lloyd's Bank

3   Barclay's Bank

4   60 Market Place

5   1 Market Place

6   2 Market Place

7   3–4a Petticoat Lane

8   Marks & Spencer

9   NatWest Bank

10 13 Market Place

11 15 Market Place

12 19 Market Place

13 24 Market Place

14 27–8 Market Place

15 29 Market Place

16 The waterfront

17 Exchange Buildings

18 Assembly Rooms

19 45–50 Market Place

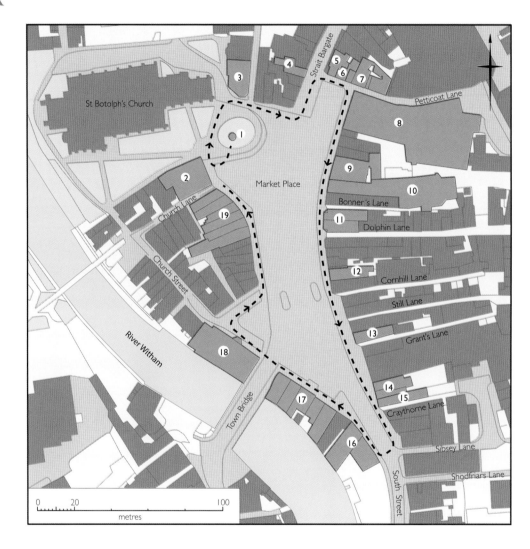

South Street and South Square walk

KEY

1   Shodfriars Hall

2   Pilgrim House

3   10 South Street

4   Custom House

5   Pilgrim Mansions

6   3–9 Spain Lane

7   Blackfriars Theatre

8   Spain Court

9   Lincoln's Warehouse

10   Magnet Tavern

11   Haven Hall

12   Riverside Lodge

13   Guildhall

14   Fydell House

15   4 South Square

16   5 South Square

17   6 and 7 South Square